Educational Resear

The OECD Handbook for Innovative Learning Environments

This work is published the responsibility of the Secretary-General of the OECD. The opinions expressed and arguments employed herein do not necessarily reflect the official views of the OECD member countries.

This document and any map included herein are without prejudice to the status of or sovereignty over any territory, to the delimitation of international frontiers and boundaries and to the name of any territory, city or area.

Please cite this publication as:
OECD (2017), *The OECD Handbook for Innovative Learning Environments*, OECD, Publishing, Paris, *http://dx.doi.org/9789264277274-en*.

ISBN: 978-92-64-27723-6 (print)
ISBN: 978-92-64-27727-4 (PDF)

Series: Educational Research and Innovation
ISSN: 2076-9679 (online)
ISSN: 2076-9660 (print)
DOI:10.1787/20769679

Photo credits:
© skynesher/iStock

Foreword

Over the last decade, the OECD region has seen a 20 percent rise in spending per school student but yet little significant improvement in learning outcomes. When other sectors see flat-lining productivity they look to innovation. In many fields, people enter their professional lives expecting their practice to be transformed by innovation. This is still not widespread in education. When the OECD conducted its first international survey of teachers, teaching and learning (TALIS), an average of only just over a quarter of teachers responded that more innovation in their teaching would be valued, never mind rewarded, in their schools.

Governments can help to open up systems to innovation. They can create an innovation-friendly climate that encourages transformative ideas to flourish on the ground, both by fostering innovation within the system and by creating opportunities for outside innovations to come in. They can help strengthen professional autonomy and a collaborative culture where great ideas are shared and refined. Governments can help to make great ideas real by providing access to funding and non-financial support to lift those ideas into action. Not least, governments can build incentives and signals that strengthen the visibility and demand for what demonstrably works.

But governments can only do so much. Silicon Valley works because governments have created the conditions for innovation, not because they do the innovation. Similarly, governments cannot innovate in classrooms. If there has been one lesson learnt about innovating education, it is that teachers, schools and local administrators should not just be involved in the implementation of educational change but they should have a central role in its design. They need robust frameworks and sound knowledge about what works if they are to be effective innovators and game changers. The OECD Centre for Educational Research and Innovation has devoted considerable energy to building such a knowledge base about innovative policy and practice over recent years. This Handbook now translates that knowledge base into practical tools for teachers and for leaders, whether in schools or at other levels of education systems. We hope it will empower them to educate children for their future, not for our past.

Within the OECD Secretariat, the author and editor of this volume is David Istance. Matthew Gill and Rachel Linden have been responsible for handling the logistics in finalising the report. The layout was undertaken by Design Media.

Andreas Schleicher
Director for Education and Skills
Special Advisor on Education Policy to the Secretary-General

Acknowledgements

Many have contributed to this Handbook, far more than can be acknowledged by name; this is to extend an inclusive thanks to all who have been involved with *Innovative Learning Environments* (ILE) from the beginning. Numerous experts and innovative sites have engaged with us in the project's different stages; our thanks to them and to the organisers of the many events in different countries which have served to hone the approaches presented in this Handbook.

ILE would not have been possible without much careful work done in the different participating systems. We extend thanks especially to the project system co-ordinators who have led and co-ordinated project activities in their different home settings.

Five systems stepped forward in ILE's latter stages as "Laboratories of Learning Change" - Belgium (French Community); Canada (British Columbia); New Zealand; Peru (Innova Schools) and South Africa (KwaZulu-Natal) – testing different approaches (especially Tool 4.1) and giving financial support. We are indebted to others who contributed financial support throughout ILE, including the Jaume Bofill Foundation.

The tool on the "Spiral of Inquiry" (Tool 1.2) was written by Judy Halbert and Linda Kaser. Anthony Mackay co-authored the teacher scenario tool (Tool 4.4). They each provided extensive comments on final drafts of the Handbook, gratefully received.

Our thanks too to Lorna Earl and Helen Timperley who wrote the OECD Working Paper on Evaluative Thinking which was the exclusive basis for the tool on evaluation in Chapter 3 (Tool 3.2).

Very useful feedback on the Handbook was offered through organised events among education leaders. In summer 2016, Judy Halbert and Linda Kaser in British Columbia organised discussion through a programme of education leaders in UBC, Vancouver. At the end of October 2016, a workshop of Flanders inspectors and principals in Brussels also gave detailed attention and discussion to an earlier draft. Particular thanks to Katrijn Ballet, Hilde Lesage and Micheline Scheys.

Jackie Talbot and Rose Carpenter, who were among the New Zealand "Laboratory of Learning Change" team, made valuable suggestions on the learner agency tool (Tool 1.3).

We are particularly grateful for the expert guidance provided by Valerie Hannon and Anthony Mackay throughout ILE and related innovation events, which sharpened significantly its concepts and approaches.

Mariana Martinez-Salgado, formerly the ILE project officer, made an invaluable contribution on many aspects of this Handbook and provided extensive feedback and design inputs. Emily Heppner, formerly project administrator, also provided useful feedback and detailed editing, as well as important logistical support.

We are grateful for the active encouragement and advice of the Centre for Educational Research and Innovation (CERI) Governing Board in the development of this resource. At the suggestions of two Board members [Helen Ängmo (Sweden), Gábor Halasz (Hungary)], two new tools were added - on learners and partnerships.

We also wish to thank our colleagues in CERI, in the EDU Communications team and in PAC, in particular Anne-Lise Prigent for her helpful editorial advice.

Table of contents

Figures

Acronyms and abbreviations

CERI: The Centre for Educational Research and Innovation at OECD.

EDU: The Directorate for Education and Skills at OECD.

Formative cycle/formative learning leadership: the systematic use of evidence about learning achievements, gains etc. to inform educational strategies and leadership.

ICT: Information and Communication Technology.

ILE: The OECD project (and its publications), "Innovative Learning Environments".

Innovation (for the ILE project): fresh ways of meeting outstanding challenges in a spirit of openness to disciplined experimentation.

Learning ecosystem: diverse providers, resources and learners operating as an organic unit in interaction with its environment and with other ecosystems.

Learning environment: organised learning for given groups of learners around a single pedagogical core and shared learning leadership.

Learning leadership: the human agency shaping learning within schools, other environments and ecosystems through a set of Ds – drive, direction, design and dialogue.

Meso level: networks, communities, chains and initiatives lying between learning environments, on the one hand, and the more aggregated "meta level", on the other.

Meta level: covers all the learning environments and meso-level arrangements within whatever system boundaries are appropriate.

OECD: The Organisation for Economic Co-operation and Development.

PAC: The Public Affairs and Communications Directorate at OECD.

Pedagogical core: the elements, relationships and dynamics about learning and teaching at the heart of each learning environment.

PISA: The OECD Programme for International Student Assessment, triennial testing of 15-year-old students in many different countries.

STEM: Science, technology, engineering and mathematics.

TALIS: The OECD Teaching and Learning International Survey.

The "7+3" framework: combines the 7 Learning Principles with 3 innovation dimensions around the pedagogical core, learning leadership and partnerships.

Executive summary

This Handbook is the culmination of the *Innovative Learning Environments* (ILE) project run over the decade since the mid-2000s. The Handbook is aimed at those working in education leadership, policy and practice looking for succinct frameworks and practical tools to help them to innovate in their own settings.

The Handbook is divided into four chapters. Each one is introduced by an overview section offering a concise, non-technical summary of a substantial body of international reflection on learning and innovation, underpinned in each case by a full publication, (plus other papers). Each chapter then presents practical tools, promoting through practical action ILE's key conclusions by shaping educational leadership, self-review and professional development.

The Principles of Learning to design learning environments

The first chapter presents the Learning Principles that concluded the 2010 ILE report *The Nature of Learning: Using Research to Inspire Practice*. These Principles maintain that learning environments should: make learning and engagement central; view learning as social and often best done collaboratively; be highly attuned to learners' emotions; reflect individual differences; be demanding for all while avoiding overload; use broad assessments and feedback; and promote horizontal connectedness. The chapter also recasts these Principles around teachers and educators as distinct from students to emphasise the importance of teacher learning and practice in achieving the Learning Principles.

Tool 1.1 *How well do we embed the Learning Principles?* This tool allows interrogation of how well schools and other learning environments embody what makes young people learn best.

Tool 1.2 *Building on the Learning Principles through a Spiral of Inquiry.* This tool also uses the ILE Learning Principles but with a method - the "Spiral of Inquiry" as developed in British Columbia, Canada – that structures questions, dialogue, enquiry and research in sequence.

Tool 1.3 *Learners at the centre – what do they think?* This tool involves the juxtaposition of the perceptions of staff about learners with the views of learners themselves.

Tool 1.4 *Teacher-focused to be learning-centred.* This tool recasts the principles so that they are focused on the teachers and educators, in which their own learning (as well as that of the students) is fundamental to the success of the learning environment.

The OECD "7+3" framework

This chapter overview presents the framework first published in the 2013 ILE report *Innovative Learning Environments*. It is called "7+3" because it combines the 7 Learning Principles with 3 fundamental arenas of innovation – the pedagogical core, learning leadership and partnerships. The chapter uses the framework to understand the potential of technology.

Tool 2.1 *How well are we implementing the ILE framework?* The purpose is to gain a rapid overview of learning arrangements and organisation in answer to the question "how innovative and powerfully learning-focused is our school/learning environment?"

Tool 2.2 *How can we innovate our pedagogical core?* This tool is for those schools and other learning environments ready for fundamental innovation in their teaching and learning, getting right into both the elements and the dynamics of the pedagogical core.

Tool 2.3 *Getting the most from our partners.* The purpose of this tool is to invite a learning environment, cluster or district to scrutinise its relationship with different partners and to consider how best to build future relationships.

Tool 2.4 *Tapping into the multiple possibilities of technology.* This tool pushes users to chart in detail how they currently embed and use technology and invites them to identify a technology strategy in the service of innovating learning.

Learning leadership and evaluative thinking

Learning leadership is discussed around interrogatives about such leadership: Why? What? Who? When? Where? How? The chapter also presents the guiding orientations concluding the 2013 report *Leadership for 21st Century Learning*. These maintain that learning leadership is critical for reform and innovation. It is about engaging in the design, implementation and sustainability of powerful innovative learning environments. It puts creating the conditions for 21st century learning and teaching at the core of leadership practice. It requires creativity and often courage, and models 21st century professionalism. Learning leadership is social and connected and the more that learning environments innovate, the more learning leadership will come from diverse partners often viewed as "external" to education. Indeed, transformative learning leadership involves complex multi-level chemistry, including at the system level.

Evaluative thinking is conceived as a series of steps with feedback loops (rather than once-and-for-all): defining the innovation; multiple stakeholders, different contexts; identifying the purpose(s) of evaluation; getting on with it; framing evaluation questions; collecting fit-for-purpose evidence; organising and analysing the evidence; making sense of it all; interpretation as building knowledge; and capturing and mobilising the new knowledge.

Tool 3.1 *Towards shared and formative learning leadership.* This tool offers a set of lenses for addressing how far the leadership is focused on learning and its strategies informed by learning evidence.

Tool 3.2 *Evaluating educational innovation.* This tool is about applying a series of evaluative processes: refining important issues and rationales; identifying what the evaluation will address and the best means to do this; and gathering, analysing and interpreting the evidence.

Transformation and change in learning ecosystems

The chapter overview draws especially on the 2015 ILE publication *Schooling Redesigned: Towards Innovative Learning Systems*. It presents the case for re-thinking learning ecosystems, describes features of innovation strategies and initiatives, offers the means for depicting networked learning ecosystems and presents a set of scenarios for the future of the teaching profession.

Tool 4.1 *Explaining why our initiative will work.* This tool is designed for those with an innovation strategy/initiative in place, giving a method for interrogating the theory of action behind the strategy in terms of changing learning and how the strategy is expected to lead to the desired innovation.

Tool 4.2 *How advanced is our system towards the "7+3" framework?* This tool gives a set of broad indicators through which to interrogate how much progress an education system is making towards innovation and change.

Tool 4.3 *How horizontally connected is our system?* This tool gives stakeholders the means of mapping dynamic learning systems, bringing together vertical levels and horizontal relationships.

Tool 4.4 *Teachers in learning futures.* This tool uses four scenarios to invite users to think of who will be teaching and educating in 2030, the desirability of different futures and how to move towards preferred scenarios.

Introductory **overview**

The Introductory Overview explains the origins and purpose of the ILE Handbook, and how it is based on the entire *Innovative Learning Environments* project run over the decade since the mid-2000s. It outlines how it is a practical resource aimed at those in education leadership, policy and practice. The concepts, assumptions and terms specific to ILE are presented, as is the way the project has been organised.

The four main chapters in the Handbook are outlined briefly: the ILE Learning Principles; the "7+3" framework; learning leadership and evaluative thinking; and transformation and change. Each chapter is introduced by a concise, non-technical summary of the theme plus a set of practical tools, intended to guide leadership, self-review and professional development. The Introductory Overview concludes by describing how the Handbook is located in a rich tradition of OECD/CERI work on innovation.

This Handbook is the culmination of the *Innovative Learning Environments* (ILE) project run over the decade since the mid-2000s from the Centre for Educational Research and Innovation (CERI) at OECD. The Handbook is aimed at those working in education leadership, policy and practice who are looking for succinct frameworks and practical tools to help them to innovate in their own settings.

Each of the four chapters in this Handbook is introduced by an overview section offering a concise, non-technical summary of a substantial body of international reflection on learning and innovation. Each chapter is underpinned by a full publication, plus other papers. We intend these overviews to be useful in their own right, as well as providing introductory texts to the accompanying tools.

Each of the chapters goes on to present a set of practical tools, intended to guide leadership, self-review and professional development. In a small number of cases, these have been prepared by others working closely with the ILE project. The tools themselves are broadly conceived so as to be useful to different audiences, for different purposes, in different settings. Because of this range, we do not offer detailed advice on how to use them and with what kind of facilitation. They differ too in the time foreseen to get the most from them, from the explicitly long term to those that can be exploited in a single workshop session, with others in between.

Concepts and terms in ILE

ILE has been grounded in a set of assumptions that has served both as a philosophical approach and as a frame to organise the different strands of operational work. *First,* we have based ILE firmly in knowledge about how people learn and the circumstances in which they do this most powerfully. *Second,* we have compiled and been inspired by concrete innovative cases, and have used these to inform framework development. *Third,* we have sought not only to identify desirable features of learning environments but have addressed how those features might be fostered, especially through learning leadership. *Fourth,* we moved beyond individual cases to ask how to grow, spread and sustain innovative practice at greater scale.

For ILE, a "learning environment":

- is an organic whole embracing the experience of organised learning for given groups of learners around a single "pedagogical core" (explained below); it is larger than particular classes or programmes

- includes the activity and outcomes of learning, rather than being just a location where learning takes place

- enjoys a common leadership making design decisions about how best to optimise learning for its participants.

We have been open to different understandings of "innovation" in all the systems, schools and settings that have contributed to the ILE study. We did not impose a single OECD definition on what we consider innovative practice which would have been far too restrictive and "top-down" and fail to recognise innovation's dependence on what it is trying to do and in which context. In avoiding being categorical about innovative practices, we have operated with a general, open understanding of innovation summed up as: *fresh ways of meeting outstanding challenges in a spirit of openness to disciplined experimentation.*

The Handbook is divided into four chapters, each sub-divided into overview and tools. Four main ILE publications were prepared between 2010 and 2015 and each underpins a chapter in this Handbook. These are:

- *The Nature of Learning: Using Research to Inspire Practice, 2010*
- *Innovative Learning Environments, 2013*
- *Leadership for 21st Century Learning, 2013*
- *Schooling Redesigned: Towards Innovative Learning Systems, 2015.*

The OECD has also published a number of official Education Working Papers from the project. One of these, by Lorna Earl and Helen Timperley on Evaluative Thinking, is the source for the treatment of evaluation in Chapter 3. All of these came after an initial report published in 2008 that served to scope the broad terrain (with the title *Learning to Innovate, Innovating to Learn*).

The Principles of Learning

The first chapter presents the Learning Principles themselves, and it also recasts around teachers and educators. These Principles maintain that learning environments should: make learning and engagement central; ensure that learning is understood as social; be highly attuned to learners' emotions; reflect individual differences; be demanding for all while avoiding overload; use broad assessments and feedback; and promote horizontal connectedness.

There are four tools in this chapter:

- **Tool 1.1** *How well do we embed the Learning Principles?*
- **Tool 1.2** *Building on the Learning Principles through a Spiral of Inquiry.*
- **Tool 1.3** *Learners at the centre – what do they think?*
- **Tool 1.4** *Teacher-focused to be learning-centred.*

The "7+3" framework

This chapter presents the framework first published in the 2013 ILE report *Innovative Learning Environments*. It is called "7+3" because it combines the 7 Learning Principles with 3 fundamental arenas of innovation: the pedagogical core, learning leadership and partnerships. The chapter uses the framework to understand different aspects of technology.

There are four tools in this chapter:

- **Tool 2.1** *How well are we implementing the ILE framework?*
- **Tool 2.2** *How can we innovate our pedagogical core?*
- **Tool 2.3** *Getting the most from our partners.*
- **Tool 2.4** *Tapping into the multiple possibilities of technology.*

Learning leadership and evaluative thinking

Learning leadership is discussed around interrogatives about such leadership: Why? What? Who? When? Where? How? The chapter also presents the guiding orientations concluding the 2013 report *Leadership for 21st Century Learning*. Evaluative thinking is presented as a series of steps which are continuous rather than one-off. These are: defining the innovation; multiple stakeholders, different contexts; identifying the purpose(s) of evaluation; getting on with it; framing evaluation questions; collecting fit-for-purpose evidence; organising and analysing the evidence; making sense of it all; interpretation as building knowledge; and capturing and mobilising the new knowledge.

There are two tools in this chapter:

- **Tool 3.1** *Towards shared and formative learning leadership.*
- **Tool 3.2** *Evaluating educational innovation.*

Transformation and change

The chapter draws especially on the 2015 ILE publication *Schooling Redesigned: Towards Innovative Learning Systems*. It presents the case for re-thinking learning ecosystems, describes features of innovation strategies and initiatives, offers the means for depicting networked learning ecosystems, and presents a set of scenarios for the future of the teaching profession. These four are: "Teachers in educational monopolies", "Specialist professionals as hubs in schools", "A system of licensed flexible expertise" and "In the open market".

There are four tools in this chapter:

- **Tool 4.1** *Explaining why our initiative will work.*
- **Tool 4.2** *How advanced is our system towards the "7+3" framework?*
- **Tool 4.3** *How horizontally connected is our system?*
- **Tool 4.4** *Teachers in learning futures.*

ILE in the longer stream of OECD innovation analysis

This Handbook is at the confluence of different streams and methods. Our focus is deliberately on learning – innovating learning environments and learning ecosystems – while targeting those within education who can make a difference by transforming the learning that goes on in their schools and systems.

Our practical ambition has consequences for methods of work and this Handbook is an unusual output for OECD/CERI. The Handbook's practical format as an aide to positive change reflects the importance of balancing the analysis of innovation with the provision of tools to facilitate such change. With the *Innovative Learning Environments* project we have been able to profit from a wide range of relevant analysis – from the nature of learning, to innovative cases, to leadership, to strategies and policies. We hope that this Handbook as a practical resource will help guide educators in many different communities and countries to engage in disciplined innovation.

Finally, we can locate the ILE Handbook in the long-running dedication of the OECD through CERI to understanding and promoting innovation. From the decade 1998 to 2008, the *Schooling for Tomorrow* project created scenarios and worked with futures thinking in systems. In the following decade with Innovative Learning Environments, the focus shifted to learning and came much closer to schools and classrooms, while linking back especially into the "meso" network level. Now in 2017 CERI has launched a new study on *Innovative Pedagogies for Powerful Learning* to take the innovation endeavour even more deeply into heart of the matter – teaching and learning.

In this context, the ILE Handbook is not the end point of a corpus of reflection even if it is the final product of a particular international study. It is one resource in the rich mix of analyses and reflections that we hope will inspire innovative change and suggest ways in which this might be done.

The principles
of learning
to design learning
environments

The overview section presents: a) the Learning Principles themselves, b) the Principles recast around teachers and educators. These Principles maintain that learning environments should: make learning and engagement central; ensure it is understood as social; be highly attuned to learners' emotions; reflect individual differences; be demanding for all while avoiding overload; use broad assessments and feedback; and promote horizontal connectedness. Tool 1.1 gets learning environments to interrogate how well they are organised so as to optimise young people's learning, using either a relatively rapid scan or more profound review. Tool 1.2 builds on the Learning Principles through a Spiral of Inquiry as developed in British Columbia, Canada. Tool 1.3 puts learners centre stage by getting schools to juxtapose the perceptions of staff with the views of learners themselves. Tool 1.4 recasts the Learning Principles so that they are focused on the educators, leading to the identification of priorities and strategies for action.

1.1 The ILE Learning Principles in brief

Learning research should deeply inform educational policy and practice. In order to embed the close understanding of learning in the *Innovative Learning Environments* (ILE) study, the OECD commissioned authoritative research reviews by prominent experts on different aspects of learning and asked them to identify what this showed for the design of learning environments (Dumont et al., 2010). We then distilled the conclusions from these different reviews into the seven Learning Principles presented below.

Identifying the fundamentals of learning provides the design principles to shape both individual learning environments and wider systems. Therefore, these principles are proposed as fundamental to all schools and learning settings as offering the building blocks of design, improvement and innovation.

The force and relevance of these learning principles do not reside in each one taken in isolation - they are not a menu from which to "cherry pick" some favourites while ignoring the rest. They add up to a demanding framework as the OECD proposes that all of them should inform practice and design, whether in schools or in wider settings and systems.

It is, however, unrealistic for a school or district to start working on all seven principles with equal priority at the same time. Instead, working on one or two – on engagement and emotions, say, or personalisation or formative feedback or horizontal connectedness – can provide the channel through which to drive the others. The tools outlined in this chapter recognise this need for prioritisation.

LEARNING PRINCIPLE ONE:

The learning environment recognises the learners as its core participants, encourages their active engagement and develops in them an understanding of their own activity as learners.

This principle means that learning should be at the front and centre. The learning environment should actively engage *all* students and develop in them the capacity to understand themselves as learners with the necessary strategies to be able to learn more effectively. This principle means that "learning centredness" should permeate the priorities of the learning organisation, whether it is a school or another site for learning.

The second key aspect of this learning principle is engagement: if students are not engaged how can they meaningfully learn? This is about *each individual learner* engaging and ensuring that all learners are engaged. The principle also stresses that learners should be capable of organising and monitoring their own learning, and able to assess what they have already accomplished and what still needs to be done.

When this principle is seriously informing practice system-wide, we would expect that teachers would locate student learning, learner engagement and success consistently at or near the top of their professional priorities. We would expect teachers to be knowledgeable about the nature of children's and young people's learning and to grow more knowledgeable as they gain experience. As young people come to understand themselves as learners they would become articulate about the nature and activity of their own learning and that of their peers. Other members of the learning community should be able to articulate the centrality of young people's learning, reinforced by the quality assurance system.

LEARNING PRINCIPLE TWO:

The learning environment is founded on the social nature of learning and actively encourages well-organised co-operative learning.

Learning depends on interacting with others, though there will always be an important place for personal study. Those others may be teachers or other educators and/or peers. The interaction may be face-to-face or at a distance. It may be through different media. It may also involve community learning, including inter-generational contact with seniors.

Studies have demonstrated the robust effects of co-operative forms of learning when it is done well. The co-operation needs to be designed to enable learning by all and not only the most active in the group: it should be much more than simply letting young people talk and share tasks. It may be supported by communication technologies through discussion boards, blogs, forums, chat-rooms and messaging. The ability to co-operate and learn together should be fostered as a "21st century competence", quite apart from its demonstrated impact on measured learning outcomes.

When this principle is seriously informing practice system-wide, we would expect learning environments to be alive with the "buzz" of collegial activity and learning, though not necessarily all the time. Learning spaces, building layout, seating arrangements and the like would also reflect preparedness for group work. We would expect enquiry, problem-solving and project-based pedagogies to all be widespread.

LEARNING PRINCIPLE THREE:

The learning professionals within the learning environment are highly attuned to the learners' motivations and the key role of emotions in achievement.

Learning should not be understood as a purely cognitive activity as students' emotions and motivations are integral to its success. Students are not only more motivated to work hard and to engage when the content is meaningful and interesting to them but they learn better when they feel competent and experience positive emotions. Being attuned to one's emotions is an integral part of developing personal strategies for successful learning. Using technology in co-operative, inquiry-based or community learning is effective partly because of its capacity to engage learners.

Being highly attuned to motivations and emotions is not an exhortation to be "nice" – misplaced encouragement in any case does more harm than good – but is first and foremost about making learning more effective.

When this principle is seriously informing practice system-wide, educators and others in learning communities will be articulate about emotions. We would expect that educational discourse, as well as the language used by learners and their families and other members of the learning community, would reflect the understanding that emotions are an integral part of learning success. Teachers and other educators will have developed pedagogical understanding so that they know how to push young people without ridicule or demotivation.

LEARNING PRINCIPLE FOUR:
The learning environment is acutely sensitive to the individual differences among the learners in it, including their prior knowledge.

Students differ in a myriad ways regarding their abilities, competencies, motivations and emotions; they differ too in their linguistic, cultural and social backgrounds. These differences significantly affect what happens in classrooms and the learning taking place; grasping such differences is critical to understanding the strengths and limitations of each individual learner and the larger group. A major challenge for all learning environments is to be sensitive to these differences, understand the different starting points of their students and adapt learning activities to them.

Technology is an important means to individualise information, communication and materials. Formally recording individual progress, with the active involvement of the learners themselves, permits the information to move from inside the teacher's head to become more visible and useful – to the learner, to the teachers in general and to others, including parents.

When this principle is seriously informing practice system-wide, it will be reflected in the mix of pedagogical practices being exercised – shared whole-class or multi-class learning activities; targeted small group or individual learning activities; face-to-face, virtual and blended learning; school- and community-based. We would expect there to be the widespread use of formative assessment throughout learning environments. As the learning becomes more personalised, the active role of the learners themselves becomes more powerful.

LEARNING PRINCIPLE FIVE:

The learning environment devises programmes that demand hard work and challenge from all without excessive overload.

That learning environments are more effective when they are sensitive to individual differences stems also from the fact that each learner needs to be constantly pushed up to and just above their own perceived limits of what they are capable of doing. No-one should be allowed to coast for any significant time on work that does not stretch them. By the same token, simply increasing pressure to overload does not make for deep and lasting learning.

When this principle is seriously informing practice system-wide, "growth mind-sets" (as described by Carol Dweck; for instance, 2006) will predominate over the common viewpoint that student capabilities are fixed. Instead of procedures that primarily aim at sorting students, we would expect the predominance of processes for optimising learning across the whole range of achievement and interest. There will be thorough-going personalisation as educators and learning communities devise innovative ways of stretching all learners.

LEARNING PRINCIPLE SIX:

The learning environment operates with clarity of expectations and deploys assessment strategies consistent with these expectations; there is strong emphasis on formative feedback to support learning.

Assessment is essential for student learning. Students need meaningful feedback on their work, while teachers need to assess progress regularly in order to adapt and personalise their teaching. Learners need to understand what is expected of them. Accordingly, assessments should be consistent with the learning objectives rather than representing a parallel set of measures unconnected with the objectives.

This principle is about making very clear what the learning is for and how to know when it has been successfully achieved. It is also about ensuring that the assessment is sensitive to individual strengths and weaknesses. And, it is about valuing feedback so that the assessment serves the formative purpose. All this implies demanding roles for teachers.

When this principle is seriously informing practice system-wide, there will be widespread capacity to articulate the methods of formative assessment and the use of evidence. Self-review and evidence-informed learning leadership will become increasingly prominent aspects of learning systems. There will be a significant shift away from simple "pass/fail" and "right/wrong" judgements towards mastery, understanding and the capacity to transfer knowledge to new problems. These demanding expectations will extend widely beyond individual professionals and schools in a culture of high quality teaching and learning.

There will be flourishing diverse metrics in use that are able to reflect deep learning, social capabilities and what are often called "21st century competences".

LEARNING PRINCIPLE SEVEN:

The learning environment strongly promotes "horizontal connectedness" across areas of knowledge and subjects as well as to the community and the wider world.

A great deal of learning comes about through making connections and especially when learners are able to make these for themselves. Learners need to be able to integrate discrete objects of learning into larger frameworks of knowledge and curricular themes. In this way, knowledge can be built on and transferred; it can be used to address unfamiliar problems rather than just those set by teachers at a particular time.

Connections need to be made across different subjects in inter-disciplinary ways. Meaningful real-life problems do not fit neatly into subject boundaries, and addressing such problems makes learning more relevant and engaging. Connections also need to be made between the learning that takes place within schools and outside. Learner homes, the community and the wider world offer enormous potential and sources for learning. In short, learning environments need to promote "horizontal connectedness".

Putting "Learning Principle Seven" widely into practice will have meant extensive work to integrate knowledge around key concepts. There will have been a great deal of research and development around pedagogical expertise, content knowledge and inter-disciplinarity. Diverse assessment metrics and flexible qualifications that assume holistic understanding will have incentivised leaders, educators and other professionals, learners and their parents and other stakeholders to embrace horizontal connectedness. Partnerships and networks will be the norm.

1.2 The principles reformulated around educators

The seven principles, reformulated around teachers and educators offer a parallel set of lenses through which to reconsider fundamental practices. Schools should be powerful learning and working environments for teachers as well as for the students. Viewed in this light, the principles reformulated in this way suggest that learning environments and systems should be:

- places where *educators share a clear priority about the centrality of learning,* for their students but also for themselves, and are fully engaged in meeting that priority; the teachers as well as the students understand themselves as learners

- where *teaching is not viewed as a private matter* and is often collaborative
- where teachers are recognised as performing much more effectively when motivated, which in turn is *intricately linked to their emotions* (satisfaction, self-efficacy, avoidance of helplessness and anxiety etc.)
- places which are acutely sensitive to *individual differences in the capacities and experiences of teachers*
- *highly demanding for each educator* while avoiding excessive overload and stress that diminishes not enhances performance
- where *expectations for educators are clear and they work formatively* – in their assessments and teaching of learners but also through organisational design strategies that generate rich evaluative information on the teaching and learning taking place
- where there is *horizontal connectedness* to which educators centrally contribute – across activities and subjects, in- and out-of-school and with other schools, groups and organisations with which the educators are connected.

TO FIND OUT MORE

Dumont, H., D. Istance and F. Benavides (eds.) (2010), *The Nature of Learning: Using Research to Inspire Practice*, OECD Publishing, Paris, *http://dx.doi.org/10.1787/9789264086487-en*.

Dweck, C.S. (2006), Mindset: *The New Psychology of Success*, Random House, New York.

Earl, L. and H. Timperley (2015), "Evaluative thinking for successful educational innovation", *OECD Education Working Papers*, No. 122, OECD Publishing, Paris, http://dx.doi.org/10.1787/5jrxtk1jtdwf-en.

Halbert, J. and L. Kaser (2013), *Spirals of Inquiry: For Equity and Quality*, BCPVPA Press, Vancouver.

THE PRINCIPLES OF LEARNING TO DESIGN LEARNING ENVIRONMENTS: THE TOOLS

Tool 1.1 *How well do we embed the Learning Principles?* This tool allows interrogation of how well schools and other learning environments embody what makes young people learn best. This tool may be used for a relatively rapid scan, though ideally it should lead to a more profound analysis that will naturally take longer.

Tool 1.2 *Building on the Learning Principles through a Spiral of Inquiry.* This tool also uses the ILE learning principles but with a method – the "Spiral of Inquiry" – developed in British Columbia, Canada. The Spiral structures questions, dialogue, enquiry and research in sequence. It gets leaders and educators to engage in collaborative inquiry through a disciplined approach to help them design powerful learning environments.

Tool 1.3 *Learners at the centre – what do they think?* This tool puts the learners centre stage. It involves the juxtaposition of the perceptions of staff about learners with the views of learners themselves. The endeavour to gain an accurate picture of what students really think is itself revealing of how well the learning environment recognises learner voice. Making sense of the findings and their implications may well need the involvement of a third party as facilitator.

Tool 1.4 *Teacher-focused to be learning-centred.* This tool recasts the Principles so that they are focused on the teachers and educators. The innovative school demands new definitions of educator roles in which their own learning is fundamental to the success of the learning environment. The tool invites familiarisation with the Principles, choosing one as the focus for action and deciding on strategies for putting it into action.

Tool 1.1
How well do we embed the Learning Principles?

This tool offers a vehicle for asking searching questions about how well schools and other learning environments are based on what makes young people learn best. This may be in a single school. It may be a group of schools asking this question collectively. It may be a district (in which case replace "your school" by "your schools"). It need not be restricted to schools – a community learning project will find this tool just as relevant as will a school.

The tool may be used for a relatively rapid scan or for a more profound in-depth analysis. It will work best with a more in-depth analysis but the simpler review will still allow you to scan your school in terms of the learning principles – Steps One and Two – and provide a basis for moving forward.

The more in-depth exercise involves gathering evidence and deciding on action to be taken based on your analysis. It is also about following up on your actions to see how much better the learning principles are being put into practice as a result.

There are further basic choices for you to make in applying the tool. One choice is whether you feel it is more important to focus on the areas that are already strengths or instead on the principles that are the least well implemented in your school. There is the choice about whether to concentrate on all principles through a particular focus such as writing or number or verbal articulation or inquiry, rather than make everything a priority. Normally, you will need to prioritise.

Step One: Familiarisation with the Learning Principles

The first step is to discuss the meaning of these principles. It is not about how well they apply in your situation – this comes next. It is about making sure that everyone understands them. You'll find them in the introductory text. It involves reading them – in advance or as an exercise to do together – but it is especially about taking the time to discuss them.

Step Two: Overviewing the existing situation

This is now the time to ask collectively – a leadership group or a whole staff or school community – how well you think you are putting these principles into practice. As we stressed in the introductory text, we see these as needing to be considered as a whole set. While later you may prioritise, at this stage you

Tool 1.1 How well do we embed the Learning Principles? **(continued)**

should ask about how well all seven principles inform your practice. For your school, district or cluster:

- *How far is each principle reflected in your visions, plans and designs?* Place the numbers 1 – 7, corresponding to each of the Learning Principles, in the top half of the chart (Figure 1.1): are they sufficiently prominent or not enough?

- *How well is each principle being achieved in practice,* including how well it reaches all targeted learners? Now place the numbers 1– 7 in the lower half of the chart corresponding to "achievements in practice".

Take time to discuss the placements and why you have chosen these. Note disagreements about the placements but if possible seek a consensus viewpoint.

Figure 1.1. Grid for locating the application of the ILE principles

	Degree of application of the learning principles	
	Well or Very Well	Still Far From Enough
Intentions, plans and designs		
Achievements in practice		

Step Three: Gathering the evidence

List the kinds of evidence that will support the assessments of how well you are meeting the different learning principles, both in designs and in achievements in practice. Discuss how adequately the evidence identified will capture the placements. This has a double function: clarifying what you would like to know about the learning taking place and identifying the means to support your opinions.

Next, embark on gathering the available evidence to support these judgements. This process may well take time. If there are disagreements about the extent to which the school or schools are realising particular learning principles, your evidence may well resolve the question of which of the competing viewpoints is most plausible. (If this evaluative work starts to take on greater significance you may need to do it more systematically as with Tool 3.2).

Then, having gathered evidence:

- *Revisit the original placements* of the numbers on the chart in the light of the evidence: discuss whether they should be maintained and revise if necessary. Seek to resolve any disagreements in the original assessments.

Tool 1.1 How well do we embed the Learning Principles? **(continued)**

- Discuss the adequacy of the evidence available on how well the ILE learning principles are being met in your school/learning environment. You may decide that improved evidence should be part of your course of action (Step Four).

Step Four: Deciding on the course of action

This is a critical stage. Address the following questions:

- In the light of the review and evidence-gathering, what are the key priorities for change? Why these?

- What are your strategies to make these changes happen? Why are these strategies expected to produce the desired effects?

- (Anticipating Step Five) What evidence will show whether the desired changes are happening and how will we monitor the changes?

Step Five: Revisiting the situation

After an appropriate time period, review the progress achieved:

- If the change has been disappointing, ask: how far did we fail to implement an adequate strategy, is it too early to see results, or was our original analysis faulty?

- If change has lived up to expectations, what should we do next to sustain progress and to make more?

This tool, with its cycles of revisiting the application of the learning principles, may be applied repeatedly. In subsequent applications, other learning principles and priorities for action may become the priorities. If the ambition is to use it for more than the one-off scanning process, gathering evidence will be especially important.

Tool 1.2
Building on the Learning Principles through a Spiral of Inquiry

Another way of getting teams of educators to work together using the Learning Principles has been developed by our colleagues Judy Halbert and Linda Kaser in British Columbia, Canada, working with Helen Timperley in New Zealand. This is called the "Spiral of Inquiry" and it has been widely applied in Canada and further afield. The Spiral is a way of structuring questions, dialogue, enquiry and research in sequence. It aims to get experienced educators to engage in collaborative inquiry through a disciplined approach to help them gain the confidence, the insights and the mind-sets required to design powerful learning environments – indeed to transform their schools and their systems.

Engaging in the Spiral of Inquiry (Figure 1.2) provides participants with the experience of leading change in their own settings. Working as a collaborative team with the others embarked on a similar process in other settings builds confidence and allows joint learning from each other's experiences.

Figure 1.2. The "Spiral of Inquiry"

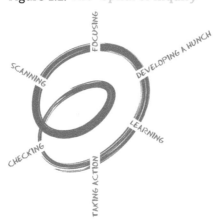

Source: Halbert, J. and L. Kaser (2013), *Spirals of Inquiry: For Equity and Quality.*

The diagram is a simple graphic showing how the phases need to be sequenced, and each phase is framed by three key questions:

- **"What's going on for our learners?"**
- **"How do we know?"**
- **"Why does this matter?"**

Tool 1.2 Building on the Learning Principles through a Spiral of Inquiry **(continued)**

In applying this tool, there should be a relentless focus on the experiences of the **learners**.

Scanning

The sequence begins by scanning the learning environment to gain a deeper understanding of the experience of the learners. The scanning process goes far beyond a simple look at available achievement data or results from satisfaction surveys. It involves asking searching questions drawn from the seven ILE Learning Principles:

- Do learners see and understand themselves as learners? Are they self-regulated? Are they becoming increasingly meta-cognitive?

- Do learners see and understand the connections across content areas?

- Are learning professionals tuned into the emotions of learners – and the connection between emotions and motivation?

- Do learners receive high quality focused feedback that provides clear directions for improvement?

- Are learners confident and comfortable in both giving and receiving feedback with their peers based on co-constructed criteria?

- Are all learners stretched through demanding, engaging and challenging work?

- Are learners engaged in high quality, well-organised co-operative learning on a regular basis?

- Is the prior knowledge that learners bring to the setting respected and valued?

- Are learners at the centre of every decision made in the school?

Scanning is all about collecting a variety of rich evidence about what is going on for learners. It is a process that takes some time. In a reasonable amount of time, generally ranging from one to three months, school inquiry teams can gather a great deal of useful information that covers all essential topics.

Sharpen the focus on a key area for change

Scanning typically raises lots of issues, but there is a limit to how many initiatives any one setting can take on simultaneously. A fragmented or

Tool 1.2 Building on the Learning Principles through a Spiral of Inquiry **(continued)**

scattered focus will result in overload and confusion. So, inquiry teams now sharpen the focus on an area for change that has high leverage while at the same time being manageable.

It is important to avoid premature decisions about what to do. Teams need to have the courage to slow down at this stage to develop a deeper understanding of what is going on in one or two key areas rather than moving to hasty action. In making the decision about where to focus, the key questions are: "What is going on for our learners?" and "How do we know?". So, it may be worthwhile to collect further evidence to know what is going on that can influence the choice of focus.

Developing hunches

The next phase involves developing hunches about the ways in which the learning professionals themselves are contributing to this situation. A "hunch" is based on intuition and not necessarily grounded in established facts.

The key point is the need to have the courage to put ideas on the table and to hear from a range of voices. This often requires courage, as it may need confrontation with well-established structures and routines that are actually contributing to the problems. The idea is get a collective understanding of the different hunches in play from those most closely involved, and these may be the learners, the leadership and/or teachers.

New learning

The "hunching" stage leads to discussion about what needs to be learnt and how this will occur as changing practice involves new learning. Designing new adult learning is the critical next step.

This phase is critical because better outcomes for learners are the result of teachers and leaders acquiring new knowledge and developing new skills that lead to new action. The main challenge at this stage is to decide on what to learn and how to learn it. It means asking why new ways of doing things will be better than what went before.

The authors warn to be wary of pre-packaged solutions, as these may well prove to be insensitive to the particular challenges of the school and learning community; they will not have involved sufficient collaborative work on the part of that community to arrive at the new learning needed.

Tool 1.2 Building on the Learning Principles through a Spiral of Inquiry *(continued)*

The authors also caution that the integration of new knowledge takes a minimum of a year of focused collaborative effort, and two years is likely to be much better. This shows that full application of the Spiral of Inquiry is not an exercise to identify change that might follow in the future but a powerful means of structuring that change process itself.

New actions and checking

New learning leads to new actions. It is about taking informed action that will make a difference. The starting question in applying the Spiral is "what's going on for the learners?" If the professional learning of the previous phase does not lead to change for the learners themselves, then the movement around the Spiral will have stopped just as it was reaching its finale.

The final phase involves checking to determine how much of a difference has been made. The authors insist that the key question here is "have we made enough of a difference?" This phase is about having an informed sense of the gains to be expected from the whole process. This requires making informed guesses about the time needed to see change happen and about the evidence that will make for valid checking that enough of a difference has been made.

Tool 1.3
Learners at the centre – what do they think?

This tool, more than the others in this Handbook, puts the learners centre stage (though we hope that they are active in the others, too). It involves the creative juxtaposition of two exercises - one about the perceptions of teachers and other educators concerning learner agency, the other about the views of learners themselves. It assumes a learning environment with significant existing trust towards the learners and a readiness to build on this still more. It also will call for a readiness to confront possibly uncomfortable findings without being defensive.

We do not suggest a strict methodology for using the tool. You may well want to listen to learners for their ideas on how it should be done.

The first two exercises are not steps, which would suggest sequence. They can be carried out simultaneously. We think it best to avoid that the one influences the other, so that you are able to base your review of "learner-centredness" on an accurate sounding of what people really think. The juxtaposition will occur when these first two exercises have been completed.

Putting learners at the centre – what do we do?

This is an exercise for all the educational staff. It amplifies reflection on the first of the 7 Learning Principles. It involves gaining an accurate picture of how staff perceive that learners and learning are at the centre of the school/ learning environment.

This exercise focuses on the questions:

How far do we think learners are at the centre of our school (or other learning setting) and why? How far do our students exercise "learner agency" by making an active input and taking responsibility for learning?

Remember: this is not asking about how we wish things to be, but how they are at present. Having compiled staff viewpoints we suggest that they are put safely aside and left unchanged.

What do the learners think about the school and the learning they do?

This is all about the learners and what they think. You will need to devise ways of getting everyone to express their views on what they think about the school (or other centre or programme) and about the learning they engage in.

It should be revealing of how far young people see the school as a primary site for learning and whether they consider they learn as much or more outside school.

Tool 1.3 Learners at the centre – what do they think? **(continued)**

You will need to be creative in devising this exercise. If it is set as a standard academic test, we can expect that those who already do well will engage in it most and it will only confirm existing views. At the same time, if learners are to express themselves frankly, it will need to be clear that they can do so without any negative repercussions. As far as possible, it should avoid being personal about individual teachers.

Devising and running this exercise successfully should be regarded as itself indicative of the role of learners in your school. Gather carefully the insights you gain from conducting the exercise, in addition to what you learn from their expressed viewpoints. You will have to decide how far you want to extend the notion of the "learner" to include their families.

Making sense of the learner responses

Understanding what comes out of the learner responses will probably not be easy. They may say uncomfortable things. What they say may not conform with the ideas generated by the staff about learner-centredness. But it may also be difficult to make sense of the learner replies: it takes hard work to "dig the jewels out of the evidence" (as expressed by Earl and Timperley – see references to this chapter).

It will be preferable if you work with a facilitator to help this process. It may be, if you have a trusting relationship with another school, that the two schools conduct this simultaneously and staff members from the one act as facilitators for the other. You may wish to use a third party entirely.

However this exercise is done, the important thing is to gain a close understanding of what the learners are telling you. Part of the exercise is to ask them directly and to hear their voice.

Where next?

Now is the time to bring out the original soundings of the staff to remind yourselves of your starting point. The creative juxtaposition lies in confronting the views of the learners with the views of the leadership and educators. How far have the learners confirmed the staff views or has the sounding of the students created an appetite to view their role differently? In general, how well are we doing to engage learners and to give them genuine voice and agency?

Where you decide to go next with the insights gained and who else to bring into the conversation from the wider community is the final main decision point in using this tool. It may lead naturally to efforts to enhance learner agency. It may suggest the need for wider change, in which case we hope you find other tools in this Handbook useful for that purpose.

Tool 1.4
Teacher-focused to be learning-centred

Schools should be powerful learning and professional working environments for teachers and educators. This is not about emphasising the importance of teachers at the expense of students but it is to recognise that being teacher-focused is integral to being learning-centred. The seven Principles reformulated around educators offer a way to do this.

Reformulating the original Learning Principles around teachers and educators gives a specification for learning environments that they should be:

- places where *educators share a clear priority about the centrality of learning*, for their students but also for themselves, and are fully engaged in meeting that priority; the teachers as well as the students understand themselves as learners

- where *teaching is not viewed as a private* matter and is often collaborative

- where teachers are recognised as performing much more effectively when motivated, which in turn is *intricately linked to their emotions* (satisfaction, self-efficacy, avoidance of helplessness and anxiety etc.)

- places which are acutely sensitive to *individual differences in the capacities and experiences of teachers*

- *highly demanding for each educator* while avoiding excessive overload and stress that diminishes not enhances performance

- where *expectations for educators are clear and they work formatively* – in their assessments and teaching of learners but also through organisational design strategies that generate rich evaluative information on the teaching and learning taking place

- where there is *horizontal connectedness* to which educators centrally contribute – across activities and subjects, in– and out-of-school and with other schools, groups and organisations with which the educators are connected.

The 21st century learning environment demands educator roles in which their own learning is central as well.

Step One: What do these educator principles mean and how well do they describe our school or district?

Discuss how well these principles apply to the teachers and educators in your school, learning environment, school district or cluster. How well do some

Tool 1.4 Teacher-focused to be learning-centred **(continued)**

apply but not others? To some people but not others? Naturally, the teachers must be prominent in these discussions and should often lead them. It will also be important to engage others involved in the teaching so that the full educator voice is heard. As strategies and narratives are prepared, others from the wider learning community should be brought in, too.

Take the time to clarify what these educator principles mean in practice in your setting. This is a key aspect of this tool. But, also ascertain whether all agree that these are appropriate principles for teachers and educators; if any disagree, what are the grounds for doing so? Is this disagreement in principle or does it reflect different views about what each should mean in practice? Are particular principles more controversial than others?

Step Two: Choose one of the educator principles as the focus for action

Decide which of the seven principles should become the priority focus for change in your setting. Choose one that enjoys widespread support while being judged as strategic for making your school or district become more powerfully learning-centred.

Take time to decide which one is best for your school, district or cluster. Try to ensure consensus about this choice as it will guide subsequent action and requires commitment from all concerned.

Step Three: Decide on strategies for putting the educator principle into action and implement them

This is the critical stage of identifying which changes are needed in order to put the principle into effect, and then acting to make the changes happen. Time will again be needed to arrive at strategies that will make a difference rather than just tinkering around the edges. You will need to be open to innovation and thinking "out of the box". Each participant should be given the chance to put ideas on the table. The senior leadership will need to be fully committed.

It may be at this stage that you need to go back to Step Two if you find that the identified actions for a particular educator principle will make less of an impact than first thought.

The chosen educator principle and the strategies for putting it into practice should be integrated into the wider vision for learning in the school/district. A narrative should be prepared which spells out why and how these

Tool 1.4 Teacher-focused to be learning-centred *(continued)*

actions will be instrumental in realising the broader vision of the learning environment. This narrative should be concise and yet able to make the key arguments; it too will need to be discussed and revised.

All educators will need to be on board and stay on board. You will need to take stock at regular intervals and to confront unexpected barriers including possible loss of professional enthusiasm.

Step Four: Take stock to decide what more needs to be done and whether the exercise should be repeated

Having kept the educator community on board and after a suitable lapse of time (say, a year), discuss the progress made on the change strategy. Discuss whether the initial choice of principle was a good one and whether the strategies chosen were the most appropriate. Discuss whether they could have been more successfully implemented. Discuss the impact of the strategies not only on the adult staff but on the quality of the learning.

This may well be the time to revisit the chosen strategies and to revise the narrative. Otherwise, and if there is an appetite for more but with different directions and focus, repeat the exercise by choosing another principle and follow the four steps. Or instead, apply another tool in this Handbook.

The OECD "7+3" framework for innovative learning environments

This chapter overview presents the framework first published in the 2013 report *Innovative Learning Environments*. It is called "7+3" because it combines the 7 Learning Principles with 3 fundamental arenas of innovation: the pedagogical core, learning leadership and partnerships. The chapter uses the framework to understand different aspects of technology. Tool 2.1 allows a rapid overview by schools of arrangements in answer to the question "how innovative and powerfully learning-focused are we?" Tool 2.2 is for those learning environments ready to ask searching questions of both the elements and the dynamics of their pedagogical core. Tool 2.3 invites a learning environment, cluster or district to scrutinise its relationship with different partners and to consider how best to build future relationships. Tool 2.4 pushes users to chart how they currently use technology and invites them to identify a technology strategy in the service of innovating learning.

This chapter presents the *Innovative Learning Environments* (ILE) framework encapsulating arrangements for learning and teaching that are both powerful and innovative. We call it "7+3" because it is based on the 7 Learning Principles (Chapter 1) and three additional dimensions explained below. This chapter also discusses different aspects of technology as illuminated through the framework.

ILE uses the language of "learning environments" rather than "schools" or "classrooms" (see also Chapter 4 on the different levels as defined by ILE). This is not because we under-estimate the importance of schools but because our focus is the organisation of learning, not the institutions where this typically takes place. It is also because a great deal of learning occurs outside places strictly speaking called "classrooms" and even outside schools altogether. If you are a school, we suggest that you will get the most from this Handbook if you dwell less on the workings of the institution and focus instead on its core business – learning and teaching.

2.1 The ILE "7+3" Framework

The full framework maintains the 7 Learning Principles as fundamental to all activities and design but then adds three more dimensions to optimise the conditions for putting the Principles into practice (hence 7+3):

i.   *Innovate the pedagogical core of the learning environment*, whether the core elements (learners, educators, content and learning resources) or the dynamics which connect them (pedagogy and formative evaluation, use of time and the organisation of educators and learners), or combinations of both.

ii. *Become "formative organisations"* with strong learning leadership constantly informed by evidence about the learning achieved through different strategies and innovations.

iii. *Open up to partnerships* by working with families and communities, higher education, cultural institutions, media, businesses and especially other schools and learning environments, in ways that directly shape the pedagogical core and the learning leadership.

Innovating the pedagogical core – key elements and dynamics

We call the elements and dynamics at the heart of each learning environment as the "pedagogical core".

Four main elements comprise the pedagogical core in our framework: *learners* (who?), *educators* (with whom?), *content* (what?) and *resources* (with what?). Re-thinking and then innovating these core elements – each by itself and especially all four together – is to change the heart of any learning environment.

- The learners may be innovated by, for instance, inviting in family or other community members to become students or when learners from different sites are brought together through communications technologies.

- The profile of educators may be innovated as different experts, adults, family or community members and students take on teaching responsibilities alongside the teachers.

- Many approaches may be taken to innovating content, such as emphasising 21st century competences including social learning, inter-disciplinary approaches, or giving emphasis to specific areas such as language learning or sustainability.

- Similarly, there are numerous means to innovate resources, extending the reach of the learning environment through digital resources as well as redesigning facilities and learning spaces.

Figure 2.1. **Innovating the elements of the pedagogical core**

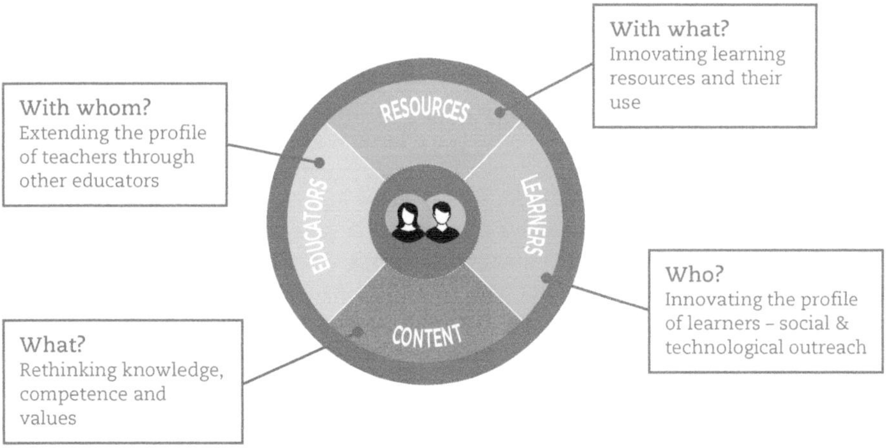

Source: Adapted from Figure 7.1 in OECD (2013), Innovative Learning Environments, http://dx.doi.org/10.1787/9789264203488-en.

The basic ingredients or elements do not operate in a vacuum but are connected dynamically. How the connections are made between learners, educators, content and resources is normally so deeply-ingrained in schooling routines and cultures that they will often pass unnoticed and are taken for granted. But they powerfully shape what happens. We focus on four forms in which these dynamics are innovated:

- different mixes of *pedagogy and assessment* that promise to engage learners, create personalisation and realise the Learning Principles

- different ways in which *educators* work in the service of these pedagogies, sometimes alone but often collaboratively in diverse forms of team teaching

- re-thinking how *learners* come together at different times in optimal ways, re-examining such basics as single age/grade practices, size of classes and how students are grouped

- re-thinking the use of *learning time*, for instance, to personalise timetables.

Figure 2.2. **Innovating the dynamics of the pedagogical core**

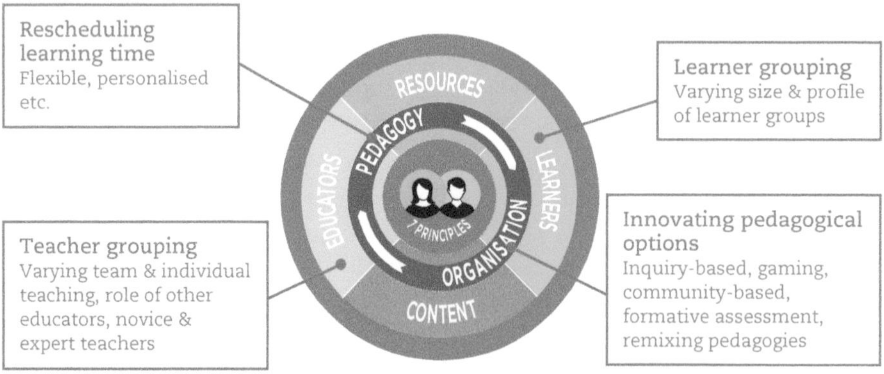

Source: Adapted from Figure 7.1 in OECD (2013), Innovative Learning Environments, *http://dx.doi.org/10.1787/9789264203488-en.*

Learning leadership and the formative cycle

Learning leadership is critical for positive change to happen. It is exercised through visions and corresponding strategies intensely focused on learning. It calls for the expert engagement of those with formal leadership responsibilities. But it is also collaborative activity, including teachers, learners and others beyond the school itself. The leadership should be richly informed by evidence about the learning taking place. These are such key aspects of change and innovation that Chapter 3 is devoted to learning leadership and evaluative thinking, and this aspect of the framework is further elaborated in Section 3.1.

Partnerships extend capacity and horizons

Creating wider partnerships should be a constant endeavour of the 21st century learning environment, looking outwards and avoiding isolation. Partners represent potentially very fruitful sources of expertise and knowledge. Partners extend the educational workforce, the resources and the sites for learning.

Working with partners is to "invest" in the social, intellectual and professional capital on which a thriving learning organisation depends. It also contributes to one of the key Learning Principles outlined in Chapter 1 – promoting "horizontal connectedness".

Such connections should include parents and families, not as passive supporters of schools but as active partners in the educational process. Partnerships may well include local community bodies, businesses and cultural institutions (such as museums and libraries). Partners drawn from higher education may be invaluable in extending the learning horizons of both students and staff and offering additional expertise for evaluation and research. As important as any of these partnerships are those with other schools and learning environments through networks and professional learning.

At the same time, especially given how professional time is so valuable and often scarce, this is not to advocate simply acquiring partners for their own sake. They need to be strategically chosen and will become genuine partners when they influence the pedagogical core, participate in the learning leadership and help to realise the seven Principles.

Figure 2.3. Partnerships enriching and extending the learning environment

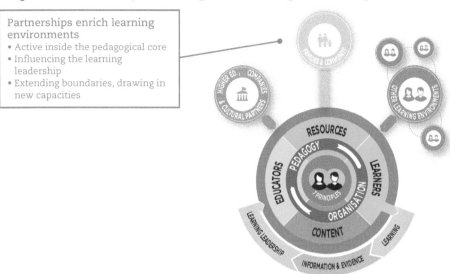

Source: Adapted from Figure 7.1 in OECD (2013), Innovative Learning Environments, *http://dx.doi.org/10.1787/9789264203488-en.*

Making learning central – the ILE Principles

Running right through the framework are the Learning Principles – the "7" of the "7+3" – as shown at the heart of Figure 2.4 and as presented in detail in Chapter 1.

Figure 2.4. The ILE Learning Principles permeate the entire learning environment

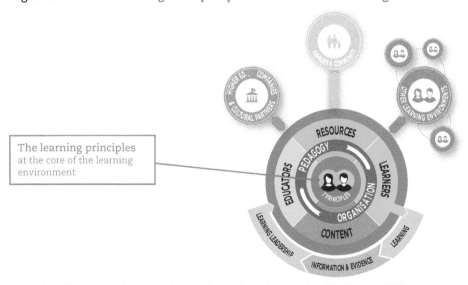

Source: Adapted from Figure 7.1 in OECD (2013), Innovative Learning Environments, http://dx.doi.org/10.1787/9789264203488-en.

2.2 The multiple roles of technology in innovative learning environments

Technology may contribute to all the different components, relationships, partnerships and principles that make up the ILE "7+3" framework. That is why we have not identified a single technology "effect" or category in our framework despite it being a clearly crucial presence in the 21st century. It is everywhere and we cannot imagine learning environments not harnessing the potential of digital technology in some way(s).

Within the pedagogical core, technology can re-define the learners (e.g. by connecting those who otherwise would be totally unconnected); the *educators* (for instance, the online tutor or the teacher from another school or system); as well as the *content* by opening up otherwise inaccessible knowledge or by promoting 21st century skills using the media that are commonplace for learners outside school. The *resources for learning* may obviously be transformed and become digital; technology may re-define the very notion of a "learning space" including in virtual learning environments.

Student-driven learning and inquiry, collaboration, personalisation and flexibility may all be enabled and enhanced with technology, and options like simulations or games or distant real-time collaboration depend on it. A formative organisation relies on technology to manage learning data and feedback; distributed learning leadership may depend on it for communication, as might teacher learning using online materials, collaborative platforms or social media. Options for learning design and re-design may be critically informed by exemplars available on line, including any necessary support for them to be sustained.

Communication technologies and social media represent powerful means for partnerships to flourish, whether through the platforms for parents to engage in their children's education or for teachers to engage with each other in professional communities or through offering access to expert knowledge developed elsewhere. It may be as simple as allowing partners to find each other more effectively.

At the same time, the mere presence of technology is not by itself sufficient to innovate learning environments. Nor should innovation be assumed to be synonymous with going digital, as this may only be reproducing traditional methods and pedagogies with a different format.

TO FIND OUT MORE

Dumont, H., D. Istance and F. Benavides (eds.) (2010), *The Nature of Learning: Using Research to Inspire Practice*, OECD Publishing, Paris, *http://dx.doi.org/10.1787/9789264086487-en*.

Istance, D. and M. Kools (2013), "OECD work on technology and education: Innovative learning environments as an integrating framework", *European Journal of Education*, Vol. 48/1, March.

OECD (2013), *Innovative Learning Environments*, OECD Publishing, Paris, *http://dx.doi.org/10.1787/9789264203488-en*.

OECD (2015), *Schooling Redesigned: Towards Innovative Learning Systems*, OECD Publishing, Paris, *http://dx.doi.org/10.1787/9789264245914-en*.

OECD ILE Case Studies, *www.oecd.org/edu/ceri/innovativelearningenvironments.htm*.

THE OECD "7+3" FRAMEWORK FOR INNOVATIVE LEARNING ENVIRONMENTS: THE TOOLS

Tool 2.1 *How well are we implementing the ILE framework?* The purpose of this tool is to gain a rapid overview of learning arrangements and organisation in answer to the question "how innovative and powerfully learning-focused is our school/learning environment?" It offers steps through which to interrogate your learning organisation in terms of the "7+3" frame. If you need to go more deeply, we suggest turning to other tools in this Handbook.

Tool 2.2 *How can we innovate our pedagogical core?* This tool is for those schools and other learning environments that feel ready for fundamental innovation in the organisation of their teaching and learning. This means attention to the elements and the dynamics of the pedagogical core, but also to bringing these all together, leading to the formulation and implementation of a holistic innovation strategy.

Tool 2.3 *Getting the most from our partners.* The purpose of this tool is to invite a learning environment, cluster or district to scrutinise its relationship with different partners and to consider how best to build future relationships. It is in three steps, each of which can be covered in separate sessions or they can be completed during a single retreat. The final session includes the identification of a single partner of strategic importance to be targeted in the future.

Tool 2.4 *Tapping into the multiple possibilities of technology.* This tool pushes learning environments to chart in detail how they currently embed and use technology. It invites them to identify a technology strategy in the service of innovating learning, often going well beyond the technology itself.

Tool 2.1
How well are we implementing the ILE framework?

The purpose of this tool is to gain a rapid overview of arrangements to answer the question "overall, how innovative and powerfully learning-focused is our school/learning environment?"

It involves getting the group to:

- Discuss all together the framework and clarify for themselves what it means.

- Break into working groups on each element of the framework. The different groups/sessions may best be led by those other than the principal. Try to reach consensus, or at least to clarify the main schools of thought. (Alternatively, with sufficient time, all in the learning community may want to take part in the review of all aspects.)

- Come back as a whole to bring together the main outcomes of the discussion and review an agenda for change.

The different aspects defined by the framework are taken up in more depth through other tools. So, if an area is identified as needing greater attention we suggest you consider using these next.

This tool can equally be used by networks, districts or system-level agencies with minor adjustments to wording.

The pedagogical core

The elements, relationships and dynamics at the heart of each learning environment we define as the "pedagogical core". The elements and dynamics are separated into two groups in this tool. A more detailed focus on the pedagogical core is offered through Tool 2.2.

Innovating the key elements of the pedagogical core

The four principal elements identified through ILE are learners (who?), educators (with whom?), content (what?) and resources (with what?). Any one of these may be the subject of innovation, as indicated in the diagram.

Discuss these diagram questions as they apply to you. Then bring the ideas together to ask: How ready have we been to innovate the key elements of our pedagogical core as a whole in line with our overall objectives?

Tool 2.1 How well are we implementing the ILE framework? **(continued)**

Figure 2.5. Innovating the elements of the pedagogical core

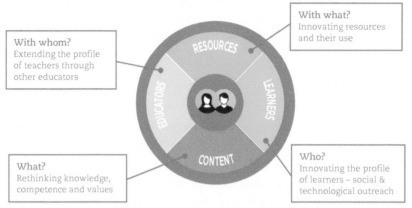

Source: Adapted from Figure 7.1 in OECD (2013), *Innovative Learning Environments*, http://dx.doi.org/10.1787/9789264203488-en.

Innovating the key dynamics in the pedagogical core

The key elements of the pedagogical core do not operate in a vacuum but are connected dynamically each to the other. This module invites you to ask about pedagogy, the organisation of learning time and how educators and learners are grouped in their educational work.

Figure 2.6. Innovating the dynamics in the pedagogical core

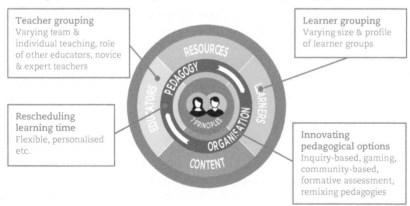

Source: Adapted from Figure 7.1 in OECD (2013), *Innovative Learning Environments*, http://dx.doi.org/10.1787/9789264203488-en.

Tool 2.1 How well are we implementing the ILE framework? **(continued)**

Ensure that the group is familiarised with the diagram and the concepts involved, as they apply to your school or learning environment. Discuss your current practice in relation to the four dynamics. Then bring the ideas together to ask: "How ready have we been to innovate the key dynamics of our pedagogical core in line with our overall objectives?"

Learning leadership and the formative cycle

This module is about how the learning leadership is exercised, what knowledge about learning is being generated and how this feeds back formatively to the learning leadership to enable innovation and re-design. (More detailed treatment is offered through Tool 3.1.)

Discuss the diagram and get familiarised with learning leadership and the formative cycle. Then, address the following questions:

- How much is leadership focused on improving learning and who is influential in making decisions about teaching and learning?

- What are our learning visions and strategies and are they bold enough?

- How well do we capture evidence on learning and how well do we use it to inform our leadership decisions?

Figure 2.7. The learning leadership formative cycle

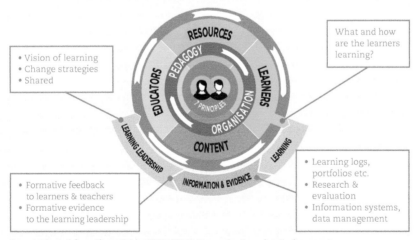

Source: Adapted from Figure 7.1 in OECD (2013), Innovative Learning Environments, http://dx.doi.org/10.1787/9789264203488-en.

Tool 2.1 How well are we implementing the ILE framework? *(continued)*

Partnerships to extend capacity and horizons

The contemporary learning environment needs strong connections so as to extend its boundaries, resources and learning spaces. Partners include parents and families, local community bodies, businesses, media groups and cultural institutions (e.g. museums and libraries) and higher education institutions. A key set of partners is represented by other schools and learning environments – working in pairs or more widely through networks and communities of practice.

A more detailed focus on partnerships is provided through Tool 2.3.

Figure 2.8. Learning-focused partnerships

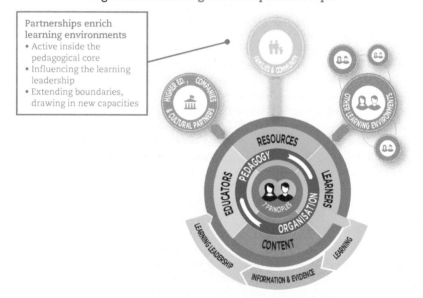

Source: Adapted from Figure 7.1 in OECD (2013), Innovative Learning Environments, *http://dx.doi.org/10.1787/9789264203488-en.*

Consider the notion of partnership and how far the school or learning environment can be said to be positive towards building connections to different partners. Then, address the following questions:

- Are parents and families genuine partners? What more could we do to engage with them?

Tool 2.1 How well are we implementing the ILE framework? *(continued)*

- Who do we work with most as partners? Do they contribute to our learning vision and strategy?

- How well connected are we to other schools and learning environments and how could we get better connected?

Bringing it together through the ILE Principles of Learning

As the purpose of this tool is to get an overview of how your school/learning environment has moved in the direction of the "7+3" framework, the conclusions from the different group discussions relating to the three dimensions (the "+ 3") need to be brought together. As a first step, compare the conclusions from the different groups and look for points of commonality.

Running right through the framework are the seven ILE Learning Principles, i.e.:

- Make learning central, encourage engagement and be where learners come to understand themselves as learners.

- Ensure that learning is social and often collaborative.

- Be highly attuned to learners' motivations and the importance of emotions.

- Be acutely sensitive to individual differences, including in prior knowledge.

- Be demanding for each learner but without excessive overload.

- Use assessments consistent with these aims, with strong emphasis on formative feedback.

- Promote horizontal connectedness across learning activities and subjects, in- and out-of-school.

Consider the emerging conclusions from the groups addressing the three dimensions (pedagogical core, learning leadership and partnerships) in terms of putting the Learning Principles into practice. Discuss how well the school/learning environment already meets these principles, and whether change is needed. (If the overview provided by this tool is not sufficiently insightful, you may need to use other of the more detailed tools in this Handbook.)

Tool 2.2
How can we innovate our pedagogical core?

This tool permits the closer focus on the pedagogical core than the broad review offered by Tool 2.1. It is for those schools that feel the need to understand in-depth what is taking place in teaching and learning. It is for those looking to innovate based on a considered analysis of all aspects the teaching and learning relationships, rather than going straight to a particular innovative pedagogical approach. It is for those who are not in school settings at all, (say, in a community-based programme) for whom pedagogical innovation is just as important.

This tool assumes the readiness to delve deeply into current practices and to consider alternatives to ingrained habits – "the way we usually do things". Its successful application depends on looking at all the elements and dynamics, rather than one of these in isolation. It may be conducted by the whole learning community or by the learning leadership as the champions of innovation.

Step One: Are we thinking enough about our core elements?

The starting point for the interrogation is careful review of the core elements: learners, educators, content and resources. The purpose is to gain a deep understanding of who and what these elements are in your own organisation, and how they might be innovated in line with your longer-term goals.

Figure 2.9. Questions on innovating pedagogical core elements

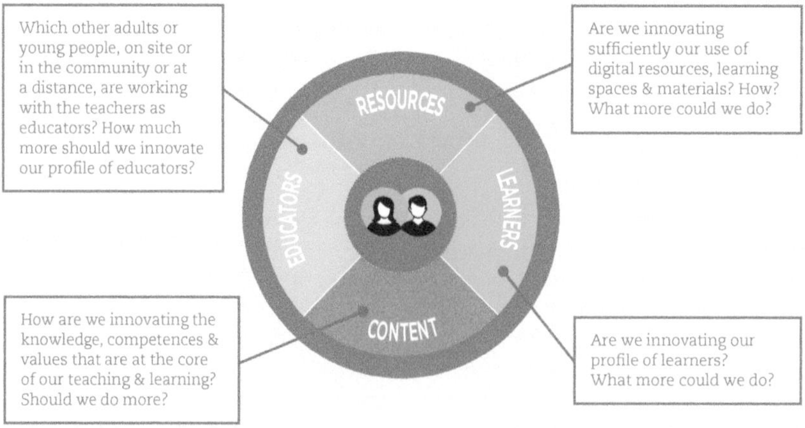

Source: Adapted from Figure 7.1 in OECD (2013), *Innovative Learning Environments,* http://dx.doi.org/10.1787/9789264203488-en.

Tool 2.2 How can we innovate our pedagogical core? *(continued)*

Address the questions in the diagram and record your answers. This cannot be done hastily, and you will need to be ready to revisit your discussions once you have engaged in Step Two on dynamics. While you may be tempted to start by breaking into groups on each of the core elements, these are fundamental questions that need everyone's consideration. Consider carefully how one element influences the others.

If there are clear differences of opinion, try to resolve them but also "agree to disagree" rather than get stuck. Come back to those disagreements after Step Two.

Step Two: What about our pedagogies and organisation?

This step raises fundamental questions of method and organisation. It needs to be closely informed by your vision of your school or centre and who you are most seeking to serve.

Figure 2.10. Questions on innovating pedagogical core dynamics

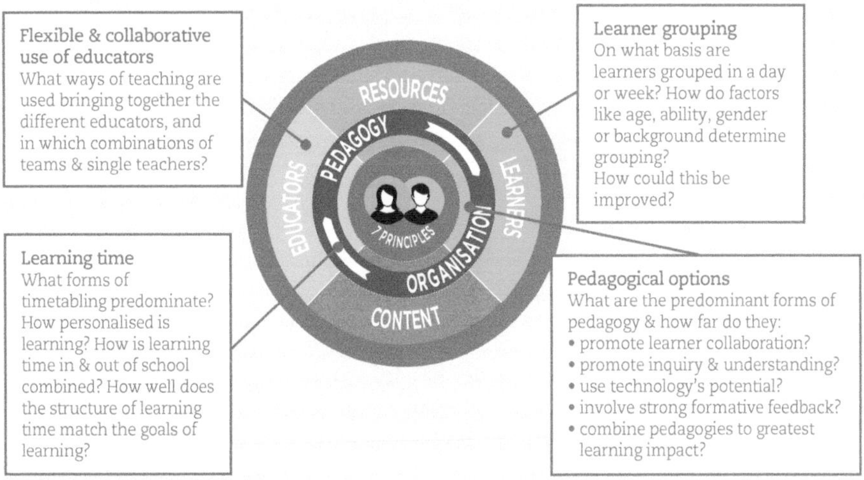
Flexible & collaborative use of educators
What ways of teaching are used bringing together the different educators, and in which combinations of teams & single teachers?
Learner grouping
On what basis are learners grouped in a day or week? How do factors like age, ability, gender or background determine grouping?
How could this be improved?
RESOURCES
PEDAGOGY
EDUCATORS
LEARNERS
7 PRINCIPLES
ORGANISATION
CONTENT
Learning time
What forms of timetabling predominate? How personalised is learning? How is learning time in & out of school combined? How well does the structure of learning time match the goals of learning?
Pedagogical options
What are the predominant forms of pedagogy & how far do they:
• promote learner collaboration?
• promote inquiry & understanding?
• use technology's potential?
• involve strong formative feedback?
• combine pedagogies to greatest learning impact?

Source: Adapted from Figure 7.1 in OECD (2013), Innovative Learning Environments, *http://dx.doi.org/10.1787/9789264203488-en.*

Address the questions in the diagram, extending to others of your own if necessary. Make sure that you cover all the boxes in order to consider pedagogy, time use and the organisation of learners and educators, rather than focusing only on one. It will also be necessary to bring them together to gain a holistic picture - they need to be coherent one with another. This cannot be rushed.

Tool 2.2 How can we innovate our pedagogical core? **(continued)**

At this stage and in the light of your review of dynamics, you may wish to return to Step One to reconsider some of your conclusions about the elements.

Step Three: Making a strategy

Now is the time to draw together all your ideas about your core activities of teaching and learning in order to innovate the pedagogical core. What will the new strategy look like? How will it be an improvement over what we do now? Most of all, how will it transform the learning of our students?

Create a narrative that sums up why change is needed and how this will revitalise your core activities in the service of your goals. Be ready to work on the narrative in more than one draft, so that it can eventually serve as a guiding statement for all concerned. As you design the strategy, ensure that all the learning community are engaged in the process.

An integral part of the strategy will be aspects covered elsewhere in this Handbook, and we suggest that you consider three in particular:

* the Learning Principles
* your partners, especially parents and the community
* evaluation and tracking of the strategy.

We are not suggesting that you use several tools simultaneously but that the overviews introducing the other chapters may usefully inform your strategy.

Step Four: Following through

Put in place a road map for implementing the strategy. Be ambitious but realistic at the same time. Consider not just the change you want to bring about but how you intend to influence those factors that will drive that change. Set milestones, anticipate setbacks and gather relevant evidence.

We think you will find the steps on evaluative thinking (Tool 3.2) helpful to guide this process even if you do not wish to follow its method in detail.

Be ready to revise the strategy in the light of experience and evidence. Be aware that innovation is often accompanied by a dip at first while it embeds before taking off. Do not let this throw you off course unless it is very clearly not working.

Tool 2.3
Getting the most from our partners

The purpose of this tool is to encourage you as a school/learning environment, cluster or district to scrutinise your relationships with different partners and to reflect on future relationships. It is in three steps, each of which might be handled in a separate session. Alternatively, all might be completed during a single workshop or retreat. It leads to the identification of a single partner of strategic importance to be targeted in the future.

As this discussion should be as frank as possible, you may decide that it is preferable not to invite your existing partners to take part. When the three-step sequence is finished, however, it will have significant implications for engaging them or for moving forward with others instead.

Step One: Who are our partners now?

Do this scoping work carefully. In the accompanying overview, we mention those partners featured most in our ILE cases, but there may well be others. Include other schools or associations with whom you network and those partners who only work with particular teachers or faculties. All teachers should take part. Be ready to revisit this partnership profile as new ones are remembered or added.

Pay attention to the educational bodies you include. Include those with whom you work collaboratively through professional choice (e.g. a school working closely in partnership with a local college to address particular student needs) but do not include offices with whom you have a strictly administrative or hierarchical relationship.

Step Two: Partners' engagement in the pedagogical core and learning leadership – How well are we doing?

It is now time to discuss the quality of the partnerships and how successful the existing partnerships are for your main curricular goals and teaching and learning strategies. Could they do more? Are there some who are disappointing and not partnering as effectively as they might? How much is that to do with you or them – are you sufficiently open to their potential contribution?

Focus in particular on the pedagogical core and learning leadership: how much are the partners involved in your core activities? Are you sufficiently networked, and are current connections integral to your main work?

Tool 2.3 Getting the most from our partners **(continued)**

Step Three: Which priority partnership next?

Focus on your main strategy for engaging students in learning and raising achievement. Might a particular partnership relationship – with, say, the local community, or a higher education institution, or other learning environments – be key to unlocking progress?

Consider both your existing partners and potential partners with whom you do not yet have an active relationship. This phase will take more time than the previous ones. It will call for the close engagement of the leadership team who will need to listen to suggestions and consider different options.

If it is difficult to address these questions because the central learning strategies are not sufficiently clear it may be that you need to apply one of the previous basic tools on the 7 Principles, the Spiral of Inquiry, or the "7+3" framework first. If so, hold onto the knowledge gained from Steps One and Two on the partnership profile. Then, return to identifying a priority partnership on the basis of this more general scanning and scoping.

Tool 2.4
Tapping into the multiple possibilities of technology

The "7+3" framework gives schools, networks and districts a way to inquire into the many ways in which technology is or could be a part of learning arrangements, rather than to see technology application as an end in itself.

Step One in this tool will give you a detailed understanding of how you are currently using technology. Step Two will stimulate reflection on specific changes needed, focusing first on what works inadequately at present and needs to be fixed. Step Three invites reflection on how technology can help you move towards fuller achievement of the Learning Principles and related strategies.

Step One: Audit of existing technology use

A superficial stock-take would only look at equipment. While that needs to be included in the audit this tool invites you to go much further.

The three dimensions – the pedagogical core, learning leadership and partnerships – should all be included, (the 7 Principles come into play later during Steps Two and Three). The questions for each feature of the learning environment or system are: *"How is technology contributing and is this stable or dynamically changing?"*

You need to take the time to build as full a picture as possible. For instance, under the first bullet point below – learners – the review may include such aspects as learner mobile phone use, digital divides among learners, technology use at home, etc. Record variations, such as when technology is prominently used by particular teachers or for particular subjects compared with when it is not. Be careful to avoid over-reporting technology use – it needs to be an accurate review. Collaborative research may be needed.

The elements of the pedagogical core:

- the **learners** (pupils, students and any others who may be actively learning, such as groups of parents or seniors, including from a distance)
- the **educators** (teachers, ancillary staff, voluntary and occasional expertise, tutors at a distance)
- **content** (curricula, coursework, knowledge and skills, including digital knowledge and skills and aspects of the curriculum that depend on digital access and use)

Tool 2.4 Tapping into the multiple possibilities of technology *(continued)*

- **resources** (this refers especially to learning and educational resources and it covers digital materials and use of space and infrastructure for learning. But it may include the financial resources invested in technology [human resources have been counted under "educators"]).

The dynamics of the pedagogical core:

- the **pedagogical mix, including assessment** – how technology is used as part of pedagogy and how information is stored and used

- how **learners are grouped** – ways that technology is used to inform or facilitate different forms of learner grouping

- the organisation of **learning time** and how this is structured or facilitated using technology

- **grouping and collaboration among educators** – how technology is used to inform or facilitate different forms of educator grouping, including how materials and student information are shared.

Learning leadership and the formative cycle:

- **visions, learning strategies and implementation:** the role of technology as a vehicle for these and how they are recorded and communicated

- **the role of professional learning** in realising the strategies, and where this is facilitated through information and communication technologies

- how the **leadership is informed about the learning taking place:** evaluation, review, information systems and how these are digitally-based

- how widely **leadership is shared** beyond senior management through ICT, especially (but not only) teachers and learners.

Partnerships extending capacity and horizons:

- **Who are the different partners,** how were they identified and how connected to the learning environment using technology? Are any of the partners specifically focused on extending digital capacity and expertise?

- The role of **networks and communities of practice,** to which the organisation or individuals within it belong, and how mediated through technology.

Tool 2.4 Tapping into the multiple possibilities of technology **(continued)**

Take time to discuss how the audit should be put together and whether it is complete. Be sure you have tapped into all relevant sources of information, including learners, and share the results with them. Do not move quickly to judge what works well and less well: the purpose of undertaking an extensive audit in Step One is to appreciate fully the current situation and to avoid a hasty diagnosis of priorities for change.

Step Two: What works well? What works less well?

Gain consensus on what works reasonably well. Discuss the reasons for coming to this positive assessment.

Then, focus especially on where digital skills, systems or use represent important barriers to positive change. These may be shortcomings in teachers' technology skills but they may extend well beyond these. Having addressed problems, check that the original assessment of what works well does not need revision.

Choose problem areas that are preventing you fully from realising the learning strategies you wish to follow. Constantly use your audit as the evidence base to inform judgements.

Step Three: Strategies to address the problems

Discuss how best to address the stumbling blocks, bearing in mind that the most effective solutions may not be technological at all. Decide how best to integrate these solutions into the larger learning strategies. Use the full audit to consider organisation-wide strategies as well as addressing discrete problems. Define objectives and possibly set targets related to the audit in terms of where you would like to be in the future.

Define a time period after which you will do a review of progress. Decide which aspects need to be monitored on an on-going basis.

When the time is reached, discuss how successfully the strategy has achieved its objectives. Decide then whether a new audit is needed and the tool repeated, or whether one of the other tools might be more useful.

Learning leadership
and evaluative thinking

The overview section is based on the 2013 ILE report on learning leadership and on an approach to evaluating innovations developed by Lorna Earl and Helen Timperley. Learning leadership is presented around responses to a set of interrogatives (why? what? who? when? where? and how?), and guiding orientations. The evaluation steps are: defining the innovation; multiple stakeholders, different contexts; identifying the purpose(s) of evaluation; getting on with it; framing evaluation questions; collecting fit-for-purpose evidence; organising and analysing the evidence; making sense of it all; interpretation as building knowledge; and capturing and mobilising the new knowledge. Tool 3.1 offers lenses for addressing how far the leadership is focused on learning and its strategies informed by learning evidence. Tool 3.2 allows schools or networks to: refine important issues and rationales; identify what the evaluation will address and the best means to address this; and gather, analyse and interpret the evidence.

earning leadership has occupied an important place within the *Innovative Learning Environments* (ILE) study, figuring prominently in the design and re-design processes of our framework covered in Chapter 2. Recognising its importance we brought together a separate report to *Innovative Learning Environments* in 2013, namely *Leadership for 21st Century Learning*.

We propose that such leadership should be closely informed by evidence of the learning taking place - hence evaluative thinking is also highly relevant. Lorna Earl's and Helen Timperley's OECD Working Paper on evaluative thinking and educational innovation followed later in 2015 and this chapter draws heavily on that analysis.

3.1 Leadership as integral to innovative, powerful learning environments

Learning leadership is critical and is one of the three dimensions in our "7+3" framework. It calls for visions and corresponding strategies intensely focused on learning. It calls for leadership as collaborative activity, in which the teachers, learners and the wider community are engaged.

The leadership should be richly informed about the learning taking place. Just as formative feedback should be integral to individual classes, so should the whole organisation use learning evidence to create strategies for learning and revise them depending on what that evidence shows. This implies strong processes of self-evaluation and the constant endeavour of sharing knowledge about learning. "Information richness" about learning strategies, students and outcomes quickly becomes overload, however, unless that information is converted into meaningful, actionable evaluative knowledge.

Teacher engagement and professional learning are key aspects of the design and implementation process. In many powerful learning organisations, students are also deeply involved in the design and implementation of their own learning – not as an alternative to teacher professionalism and leadership but as extensions of them.

The "why" of learning leadership

A basic reason why learning leadership deserves such attention is because it is *so influential of direction and outcomes*, whether in schools, clusters or broader systems. And, as *learning is the core mission of education* then it is natural to focus especially on the leadership and decision-making that shapes this core mission.

The "what" of learning leadership

Learning leadership refers to the people and decisions that drive the design of learning environments to make them powerfully effective. It is exercised through relationships and at different levels and may extend to partners outside schools. Learning leadership should not be reduced to the qualities of individuals as it is essentially social and interactive, not a solo activity.

Figure 3.1. Learning leadership and the formative cycle

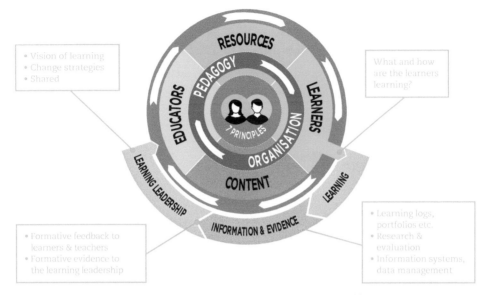

Source: Adapted from Figure 7.1 in OECD (2013), Innovative Learning Environments, *http://dx.doi.org/10.1787/9789264203488-en.*

Learning leadership is integrally bound up with the endeavour of innovation. It is needed at the different levels of any system, whether for the big picture design of structures, policies, curriculum, etc. or the detailed decisions to be made in leading teaching. Networks and communities of practice call for their own forms of leadership while contributing in turn to system leadership. And, there is leadership in the non-formal programmes outside schools that feature increasingly in the learning of young people.

Learning leadership calls for creative, strategic acts of design together with the ability to put those designs into practice. It needs resilience in the face of the messy realities of implementation. Management is thus an integral part of learning leadership. So, we would not contrast leadership with management per se but caution to avoid scenarios in which senior leaders are so preoccupied with institutional management that they neglect the core business of leading learning and teaching.

The "who" of learning leadership

There is no simple match between hierarchical position and learning leadership, and the increased organisational complexity of innovative learning environments brings more complex forms of leadership. Yet, that leadership should be shared rather than relying predominantly on the "heroic" top person. But, this does not mean to neglect the importance of *principals and other senior managers* and indeed, effective sharing often depends on the confidence and competence of the formal leader(s). In other words, it is just as inaccurate to assume that "position doesn't matter" as it is to assume that "position defines everything".

Teacher leadership, whether formal or informal, is generally exercised by influential teachers commanding professional authority. They choose to support their colleagues and believe strongly in the progress of the school and its students. Sharing leadership works in both directions: teachers helping to set broader direction but also senior managers having a say in what takes place in the classroom.

A learning community involves all its constituencies, including *its students*. The active participation of students in strategies to improve learning fosters motivation, engagement and responsibility. Far from this diminishing conventional leadership authority, it enhances it and calls for demanding professionalism.

The "where" (and "when") of learning leadership

Combining different players, levels and locations adds up to a complex layering altering the "where" and the "when" as well as the "who" of learning leadership. It is exercised within schools and beyond, at different levels, and in the horizontal network connections between learning environments. As schools innovate they often draw on partners and sources of knowledge outside the traditional school boundaries. This may be described as "anywhere" learning leadership and it increasingly needs to be "anytime" as well.

Educational discussion tends to acknowledge how much learning increasingly takes place outside formal classrooms whether through projects, peers, media or the community. The specific discussion of leadership, however, still tends to be dominated by the more familiar world of schooling.

The "how" of learning leadership

Visions, changing organisational cultures and design

Vision offers a "road map" towards a more promising future. The vision should attract partners and followers, and provide them with the motivation, suggested methods and narratives to help them engage in innovative change.

Visions need to be translated into strategies of design, which in turn need to be put into practice (referred to by John MacBeath [2013] as the "challenge of enactment"). Instead of timidity, leadership should foster can-do cultures and the readiness to take risks. James Spillane (2013) emphasises leadership as diagnosis and design with the purpose of maintaining learning front and centre. A key part of the diagnostic work is to clarify how taken-for-granted routines in schools often block powerful learning, and then to figure out how these can be supplanted by more learning-focused routines.

Professional learning

Learning is necessary both to the design task of sharpening visions and to the operational tasks of realising transformation. Knowledge strategies in schools are fundamental to any significant innovation (Elmore, 2008). Dialogue is about learning and is the means through which leadership is made explicit: educators and others in the learning community share ideas on the practices to be tried and collect evidence on their impact. The leadership is exercised through the process of inquiry (see also Tool 1.2 above).

Learning communities and networks

Creating community is an important means for visions and strategies to be shared and for developing expertise. Leadership develops and is sustained through collaborative professional learning. Networked professional communities bring together vision, collaborative learning and shared leadership. The leadership and benefits flow in both directions – from the wider community into the single learning environment and from the different sites outward to the learning system as a whole.

Orientations to guide learning leadership

These different dimensions of learning leadership imply (Istance and Stoll, 2013):

- Learning leadership is critical for reform and innovation.
- Learning leadership is about engaging in the design, implementation and sustainability of powerful innovative learning environments.
- Learning leadership puts creating the conditions for 21st century learning and teaching at the core of leadership practice.
- Learning leadership requires creativity and often courage.
- Learning leadership models and nurtures 21st century professionalism.
- Learning leadership is social and connected.
- The more learning environments innovate, the more learning leadership will come from diverse partners often viewed as "external" to education.
- Transformative learning leadership involves complex multi-level chemistry.
- Learning leadership is needed at the system level.

3.2 Evaluative thinking and educational innovation

Educational evaluation is the systematic collection and analysis of the information needed to make decisions and identify the effects of educational initiatives. Evaluative thinking is necessary to successful innovation. Rather than being unstructured, disciplined innovation involves constant problem definition, horizon scanning, analysis and monitoring of progress, the creation of contingency plans and feedback of the evidence to the innovation process and to stakeholders. Evaluative thinking thus involves a lot more than measurement and quantification.

Defining the innovation

One of the first tasks in any evaluation is getting a detailed description of what is intended. Defining the innovation – its roots, goals and philosophy – will underpin a workable evaluation approach and contribute to decisions about the innovation and accountability requirements. The goals and assumed impact of the innovation will need to be routinely revisited, informed by the evaluative evidence.

Multiple stakeholders, different contexts

Engaging key stakeholders in the evaluative thinking can substantially enhance the credibility of the innovation. Rather than telling a simple black-and-white story, stakeholders should be involved in an iterative process that takes context, culture and different viewpoints into account.

Identifying the purpose(s) of evaluation

The questions to be addressed through the innovation/evaluation process need to be clear and when they will be addressed. Defining the purposes of evaluation needs to be done directly, transparently and often. Those behind the innovation may only want to go so far with the evaluation, however - ready to engage with it to inform decision-making but uneasy about evaluation outcomes for fear of disappointment.

Getting on with it

"Getting on with it" means to develop theories of action, identify specific evaluation questions and valid methods to answer them and make sense of the findings. Innovation is emergent and needs evaluation capable of looking iteratively forward and back. Looking forward means formulating evaluative questions and collaboratively planning the evidence to be collected; looking back means considering how the evidence has been most useful in tracking progress.

Framing evaluation questions

Evaluation questions ask "what do we need to know?" These questions shape the whole evaluation process so it is essential to spend time getting these right, returning to them regularly. Internal questions may be quite different from those posed by external accountability. Questions need to provide the most relevant information for the time and context, and they should balance stakeholder needs and the intended short-, medium- and long-term outcomes.

Collecting fit-for-purpose evidence

The systematic collection of evidence provides the platform for answering the evaluation questions. The evidence must be fit-for-purpose, give an accurate representation of what is being evaluated and inform decisions. There are many ways to collect information in evaluating innovations. "Fit-for-purpose" means appropriate methods both for a valid evaluation to be made and for the practicalities of the particular case.

Organising and analysing the evidence

The next step is to decide how to organise and analyse evidence to answer the big questions. All too often analysis becomes a "fishing expedition", based on routine analyses and stand-alone statistics, whereas data analysis should not be pointlessly formal. It should make an interesting claim; it should tell a story that an informed audience will care about and it should do so by intelligent interpretation of appropriate evidence.

Making sense of it all

Insights that arise from looking at evidence need to be converted into useful knowledge to inform stakeholders and influence the innovation. Too often, much attention is given to collecting evidence, and then the interpretation is hurried and superficial. What matters are the insights that come out of the evidence, when the people who care about the innovation make sense of the evaluative evidence.

Interpretation as building knowledge

When evaluation is part of the innovation, interpretation becomes part of a cycle of collaborative knowledge-building. Learning and change arise from this deep inquiry, iterative process.

Capturing and mobilising the new knowledge

Having worked through the interpretation and knowledge-building, what emerges should be made visible and accessible to others in some accessible and retrievable form (print, audio recording, video, translations, etc.). This is variably referred to as knowledge transfer, knowledge management, knowledge translation, knowledge mobilisation and knowledge animation.

TO FIND OUT MORE

Earl, L. and H. Timperley (2015), "Evaluative thinking for successful educational innovation", *OECD Education Working Papers*, No. 122, OECD Publishing, Paris, *http://dx.doi.org/10.1787/5jrxtk1jtdwf-en*.

Elmore, R.F. (2008), "Leadership as the practice of improvement", in *Improving School Leadership: Case Studies on System Leadership*, Vol. 2, OECD Publishing, Paris, *http://dx.doi.org/10.1787/9789264039551-en*.

Istance, D. and L. Stoll (2013), "Learning Leadership for Innovative Learning Environments: The Overview", in OECD 2013b, *http://dx.doi.org/10.1787/9789264205406-3-en*.

Macbeath, J. (2013), "Leading learning in a world of change" in OECD 2013b, *http://dx.doi.org/10.1787/9789264205406-5-en*.

OECD (2015), *Schooling Redesigned: Towards Innovative Learning Systems*, OECD Publishing, Paris, *http://dx.doi.org/10.1787/9789264245914-en*.

OECD (2013a), *Innovative Learning Environments*, OECD Publishing, Paris, *http://dx.doi.org/10.1787/9789264203488-en*.

OECD (2013b), *Leadership for 21st Century Learning*, OECD Publishing, Paris, *http://dx.doi.org/10.1787/9789264205406-en*.

Spillane, J. (2013), "The practice of leading and managing teaching in educational organisations" in OECD 2013b, *http://dx.doi.org/10.1787/9789264205406-4-en*.

LEARNING LEADERSHIP AND EVALUATIVE THINKING: THE TOOLS

Tool 3.1 *Towards shared and formative learning leadership:* This tool is designed to facilitate a sustained interrogation of the leadership strategies in the school/learning environment. It offers a set of lenses for addressing the extent to which leadership is focused on learning and its strategies are informed by evidence. Ideally, we envisage that it would take several sessions to work through each module.

Tool 3.2 *Evaluating educational innovation:* This tool is about evaluation as integral to educational innovation. It suggests repeatedly applying a series of evaluative processes: refining important issues and rationales; identifying the questions that the evaluation will address and the best means to answer them; and gathering, analysing and interpreting the evidence. We suggest that all the sections get considered at the beginning, though most attention will probably focus at this stage on issues of definition and method. The tool should be used again when the specifics of data analysis and interpretation are to the fore, and yet again when mobilisation and change are uppermost, and so on.

Tool 3.1
Towards shared and formative learning leadership

This tool is based on the formulation of leadership in the ILE framework together with insights from the report *Leadership for 21st Century Learning* (OECD, 2013). The purpose is to sharpen up the understanding of the leadership that is in the service of learning, and to help develop appropriate leadership strategies. Some schools will find it useful to apply this in-depth approach after having applied the more general tools from Chapters 1 or 2.

Tool 3.1 is in six modules corresponding to the diagram below plus an additional session intended to bring together the conclusions from the different modules to decide how to improve learning leadership. Review the questions in the diagram in preparation for each module, and in each there are more detailed questions about learning leadership.

It would be helpful to identify some concrete recent examples regarding strategies and the use of evidence on learning through which to ground your discussion in concrete examples. To broaden engagement of the learning leadership team it might be advisable to use different people to chair/facilitate each module. You will need to decide how far these should include the principal and other senior managers.

Figure 3.2. The learning leadership formative cycle for schools and learning environments

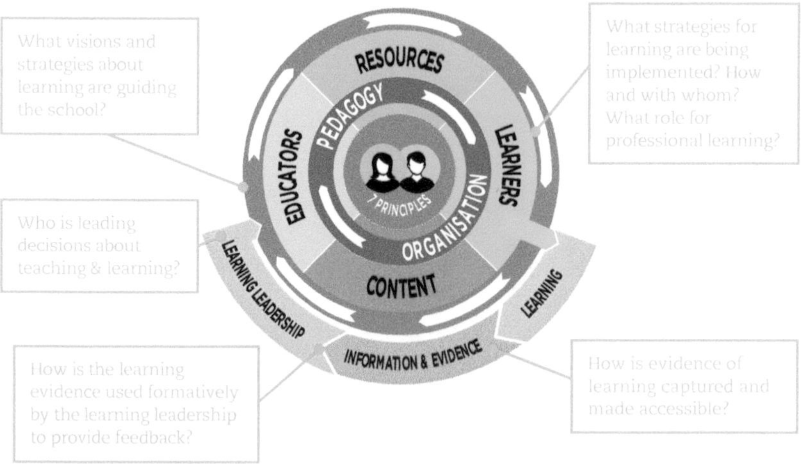

Source: Adapted from Figure 7.1 in OECD (2013), Innovative Learning Environments, http://dx.doi.org/10.1787/9789264203488-en.

Tool 3.1 Towards shared and formative learning leadership **(continued)**

The "who" of learning leadership

Focusing strongly on the nature and organisation of learning means to widen the focus so as to include but also go beyond those at the top of the management hierarchy in the organisation. The increased organisational complexity of innovative learning environments brings more complex forms of leadership but this may make effective leadership even more dependent on the active engagement of the formal leaders such as school principals.

- How far are the principal and other senior managers directly involved in decision-making about teaching and learning in the classroom?
- How widely are teachers engaged in leadership decision-making about learning? Are there designated roles for teacher leaders?
- How and to what extent are the students involved in decision-making about teaching and learning?
- Are other partners (and which ones) involved in setting direction for the school as a learning environment?

Visions and strategies

Design is critical in guiding work and change and this means the visions for learning and how these are translated into organisational strategies.

- Is there a vision guiding learning change? If so, how long has it been in place and how adequate does it seem to have been?
- How is the vision shared among all those involved in the learning community? Is it shared widely enough?
- How well has the vision been translated into strategies for change?

Building organisational capacity and community

Professional learning is an essential part of sharpening the strategic visions and of realising transformation. How are the school's organisational routines changing and how firmly are these focused on learning and innovation? There needs to be a culture of dialogue and collaboration and the creation of learning community, within the school and through wider networks.

- What professional learning has there been around the vision and what strategies for those with leadership responsibilities?

Tool 3.1 Towards shared and formative learning leadership **(continued)**

- What particular changes have been undertaken in routines and infrastructure to put the visions and strategies in place? How well have they worked?
- Are dialogue, collaboration and inquiry commonplace? Can you be described as a "learning community" and have you set out to build greater community?

Evidence on learning

Information about learning may be collected through very diverse means: one risk is that insufficient information about student learning is available but the opposite risk is of being swamped by too much so that it cannot meaningfully inform decision-making.

- What are the main sources of evidence regarding the learning taking place?
- How is the evidence on learning compiled and how robust is it? Is this done systematically?

Feedback of learning evidence to learning leadership

For the organisation to become formative, the leadership in particular must access robust evidence on the learning taking place and use it to design and re-design itself.

- How is the evidence on learning fed back to and used by the leadership? Are there any problems with ensuring effective feedback?
- How is the evidence translated into the strategic design for organising teaching and learning and how has this design been improved or innovated as a result?

Bringing it all together

- This is the session that brings everything together. It will serve as a reminder of the key points and then consider they add up to a coherent whole.
- Identify the stand-out conclusions from each module and reflect on the broad picture of how effective the learning leadership has been to date.
- If more could be done to improve learning leadership, what are the main lines of change to be put in place?
- Consider whether how effective the formative cycle works at present – from leadership decisions to strategies to evidence on learning and feedback into leadership and strategy design – and how it could be improved in the future.

Tool 3.2
Evaluating educational innovation

Evaluation should be a central part of educational innovation. Given that innovation by its nature evolves, evaluation needs to inform it along the way rather than be something that only happens at the end.

Earl and Timperley (2015) propose a sequence of evaluation questions, engaging stakeholders in the process and revisiting the questions in the light of the feedback received. This sequence covers: refining important issues; identifying the key questions that the evaluation will address and the best means to answer them; and gathering, analysing and interpreting the evidence.

This tool offers specific questions to help shape each of these stages. Even within a single school possibly unable to engage in an extensive evaluation exercise, these questions will usefully guide reflection on their innovative approaches.

WHAT? Defining the innovation

One of the first tasks in any evaluation is to get a comprehensive description of the innovation.

- Discuss and answer the following questions:
  - What do you expect from this change?
  - For whom and when?
  - What might it look like?
  - How does it work?

- Bring these answers together in a statement to describe the innovation and explain how it will bring about the desired changes (its theory of action).

WHY? The purpose of the evaluation

Defining purposes needs to be done clearly and transparently, and revisited as circumstances change. There needs to be clarity on what is to be addressed by the innovation/evaluation – "What do we need to know?" – and when the answers will be needed.

- What do we need to understand better? Who needs to know?

Tool 3.2 Evaluating educational innovation **(continued)**

- What evaluation activities have taken place up to now? What have we learnt from them and what more do we need to know?

- What do we need to know over the longer term? How will evaluation help to answer these questions?

WHO should be involved in the evaluation?

Many can be involved in the innovation, each with their own perspectives and possible biases. If the evaluation goes beyond self-review, you will need people with technical evaluation expertise, integrity and flexibility. There may well be others, and they can help (or hinder) the innovation along the way.

- Who has been implicated in the evaluation and doing what?

- How were the evaluators chosen?

- Have you made sure your evaluation is not just confirming the results that some want to find?

HOW? Approaches and methods

To gain independent review of how the innovation is unfolding means engaging a continuous cycle of generating hypotheses, collecting evidence and reflecting on where the innovation is up to. The platform of the evaluation is the systematic collection of evidence.

- What methods have you adopted for the different stages of the evaluation and are they "fit-for-purpose"?

- Are the adopted approaches the best ones for answering the most important questions you have? How do you intend to analyse the evidence?

- Are you sure that you have extracted enough from your information to address the key questions? What else do you need to know?

SO WHAT? What does the evaluation tell us?

Insights gained from evidence need to be converted into usable knowledge to inform others and guide the innovation. BEWARE: most attention in evaluations tends to be given to collecting evidence while interpreting it is often hurried and superficial.

- What does the evidence mean and what light does it shed on your initial questions?

Tool 3.2 Evaluating educational innovation *(continued)*

- Does it confirm direction or suggest changes to be made?
- What does the evaluative evidence mean for your initial "theory of action"? Were any of your initial assumptions found to be inadequate?
- Who has been involved in discussing and interpreting the findings?

WHO ELSE SHOULD KNOW? *Knowledge-building and mobilisation*

Knowledge mobilisation in innovation is a deliberate process of acting on the following questions at various points: "What do we know that should be shared with others?" and "Who should we involve?"

- How ready are you to bring others into your reflections about your innovation and how ready are you to listen to their feedback?
- With whom do you intend to share the knowledge generated by your evaluation and how will you do that?
- How ready are you to influence others who share similar situations and ambitions?

Transformation and change
in learning
ecosystems

The chapter overview draws especially on the 2015 publication *Schooling Redesigned: Towards Innovative Learning Systems*. It presents the case for re-thinking learning ecosystems, describes features of innovation strategies and initiatives, offers the means for depicting networked learning ecosystems, and presents a set of scenarios for the future of the teaching profession. Tool 4.1 gives a method for those with an innovation strategy/initiative to interrogate the theory of action behind it and how it is expected to lead to the desired innovation. Tool 4.2 offers a set of broad indicators to interrogate progress by an education system towards being innovative. Tool 4.3 gives stakeholders the means of mapping dynamic learning systems, bringing together vertical levels and horizontal relationships. Tool 4.4 uses four scenarios to invite users to think of who will be teaching in 2030, the desirability of different futures, and how to move towards preferred scenarios.

4.1 Re-thinking learning ecosystems

At the core of the learning systems for young people are schools and the systems that bind them together. More and more, these are interwoven with a rich and growing set of other forms of teaching and learning, some outside the formal system and some as hybrids of the formal and the non-formal (Zitter and Hoeve, 2012). Even within formal schooling, there are countless networks and connections that spread well outside designated roles as educators.

Growing and sustaining widespread innovative learning needs to be located in an understanding of this complexity. It has been addressed in the OECD/CERI work on governing complex systems (see OECD, 2016), which identified the need for new approaches:

> Traditional approaches, which often focus on questions of top-down versus bottom-up initiatives or levels of decentralisation, are too narrow to effectively address the rapidly evolving and sprawling ecosystems that are modern educational systems (Snyder, 2013; p. 6).

Governments nevertheless remain central to the change process because they are pivotal in determining the overall structure and distribution of learning opportunities and in generating coherence of aims, infrastructure and accountability. They have a privileged role in regulating, incentivising and accelerating change.

Too often, we think of the government role very mechanically, using metaphors such as "levers" or "scale-up" or base our thinking on assumptions of policy omnipotence within well-defined "systems". Now, more organic metaphors and models are needed.

Re-thinking levels

In ILE, with the focus on learning and innovation, we looked beyond the conventional categories of educational organisation divided into the classroom level, the school level, the district level and the system level as these are defined in terms of institutions, not learning. Instead, we distinguish:

- The *micro* level – learning resources and spaces, teaching and learning episodes, pedagogical relationships.
- The more holistic level of the *learning environment*, integrating the micro elements around organic units which share a pedagogical core and learning leadership. Learning environments need not be schools, though many of the ILE examples have been.
- The *meso* level, comprised of the many compounds of networks, communities, chains and initiatives. This level is largely invisible in formal system charts and yet it is critical for growing and sustaining innovative learning.
- The *meta* level is a summary umbrella for all the learning environments and meso-level arrangements within whichever system boundaries make sense for the question in hand.

4.2 Features of the ILE strategies and initiatives

Our ILE project brought together different strategies and initiatives for growing innovative learning, both for analysis and so as to engage systems (countries, regions, networks etc.) directly in the project (OECD, 2015).

Though the submitted cases represent only a tiny sample from the world of educational innovation, they covered widely different approaches and served to reinforce the key importance of the *meso* level. Some were organised by the ministry of education while in others the ministry played only a supporting role or else the initiative was led from elsewhere altogether, such as by foundations. Some built capacity while others were about establishing the platforms for a range of stakeholders to build their own capacity and share knowledge and practice. Some addressed particular groups of learners or had a specific content focus such as well-being or futures competence.

In *Schooling Redesigned*, we focused on three dimensions as a set of lenses through which to analyse networks and innovation:

- *Learning focused*: How learning focused is the network and how far might it be characterised as innovative?

- *The means of innovation "contagion"*: The nature of the diffusion within networks and how they spread learning innovation.

- *Formal/non-formal balance*: How informally networked are formal learning environments, how visible is the non-formal and do the formal and non-formal combine in new "hybrids"?

We look at each briefly in this section.

The nature of the learning focus

Though the strategies reported in the ILE study were already convinced of the need to grow innovative learning, they nevertheless differ in the extent to which they are explicitly learning-focused, the particular learning aims they are seeking to achieve and how they are working to put learning at the centre. Several of them make a point of identifying the learning challenge at the outset, rather than this being assumed to be known, and invite learners and their families into this process. Variants around 21st century competence define the learning aims of many initiatives, but we also had examples defined in terms of traditional cultural knowledge and values.

Different methods to diffuse the innovations

The featured strategies rely on different methods to diffuse innovation. Many of them may be found in the single "On the Move" programme in Finland. Networking and sharing information, as well as national and regional seminars, are primary channels. Good practices are shared through seminars, brochures and the website, and the programme includes in-service teacher education. The communication strategy includes the website, social media, newsletters and publications. It has been well covered in national, regional and local media, both printed and on TV and radio.

Sometimes diffusion happens when certain sites take on system leadership roles as beacons in clusters. Qualifications may assist the diffusion process through developing particular forms of expertise among practitioners and creating a community of expert practice. A further vehicle for diffusion may be through regular (often annual) high-profile events serving both as the means of communication and to strengthen the networking.

Horizontality through different combinations of the formal and non-formal

Different mixes of the formal and non-formal may be involved in initiatives to grow and sustain innovative learning. *Schooling Redesigned* distinguishes four types depending on this mix:

- formal initiatives that bring schools into clusters and networks, combining schools that otherwise would be working in isolation

- voluntary networks of schools and school-based communities of practice

- schools working increasingly with different community and non-formal bodies, whether in individual partnerships or wider clusters

- purely non-formal initiatives not operating through school institutions at all.

In our study, the cases tend to be more at the formal end of the spectrum because the education authorities were often involved in selecting them, but another project methodology would have brought a different mix.

4.3 Depicting networked learning ecosystems

What might a networked system look like at the "meta" level? Figure 4.1 combines the formal/non-formal axis with that of vertical levels to characterise in simplified terms learning systems that are more or less networked.

The right-hand column in the figures is the hierarchy of formal educational levels, (which includes some mandated school networks); the middle column is "hybrid" with schools and educators coming together in unregulated ways and non-formal players teaming up with schools, teachers and districts; while the left-hand column represents the purely non-formal players and programmes operating right outside the school system.

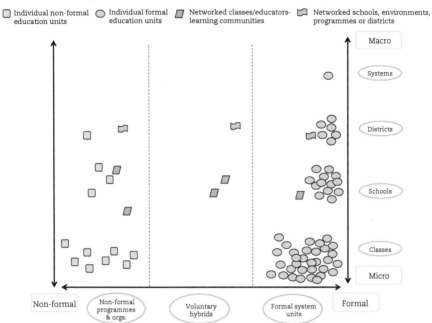

Figure 4.1. **A weakly-connected learning system**

Figure 4.2. **A strongly-connected learning system**

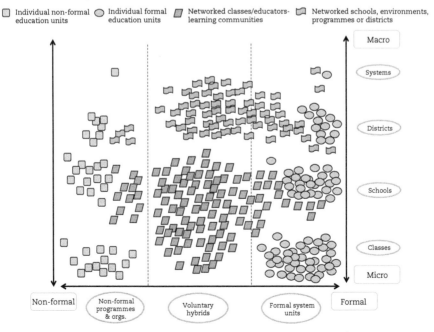

Figure 4.1 represents a hypothetical weakly-networked learning system. It is dominated by the right-hand vertical school system with few networks and cross-school communities and very little in the middle "hybrid" column. The networked learning system in Figure 4.2 depicts a very significant increase in the number of groups, organisations and programmes devoted to learning. The networked system is fuller horizontally and vertically; there are more non-formal providers, too, some of these forming their own networks totally outside the formal system, though often joining with those from schools to occupy the "hybrid" space in the middle.

What might fully-fledged "7+3 systems" look like?

What might learning systems exhibiting high adherence to the ILE framework look like? To help guide policy and practice, it would be helpful to be able to measure development towards "7+3", and this would call for a new generation of indicators focused on innovation. A first list was offered in *Schooling Redesigned*.

High engagement: In a system characterised by "7+3", there would be a cultural shift in attitudes and learning engagement, whether referring to young people or to the adults involved. There would be high levels of engagement, schools and classrooms would "buzz" and there would be very active learner voice and agency.

Collaborative professionalism: There would be a matching shift in educator views, knowledge and practice. Teachers and other educators would spend significant time engaged in professional discussion about learning strategies in general, within the organisation and in relation to individual learners. They would actively engage in learning leadership, innovation and professional collaboration, including team teaching.

Rich pedagogies, approaches and sites: There would be a rich mix and diversity of pedagogical practices, with personalised approaches and formative assessment highly visible. There will have been extensive efforts to create inter-disciplinary knowledge around key concepts and the development of corresponding learning materials and pedagogies. There would be a wide variety of sites for learning beyond conventional classrooms, more or less integrated into school organisations.

Widespread use of social media and ICT: There would be widespread use of social media and ICT, as learners engage in research and exchange around learning projects and as educators connect with each other, with learners and with other partners and networks. Teaching, learning and pedagogy will often be "tech-rich".

A dominant culture of reflection and evaluative thinking: There would be flourishing research and development around pedagogical expertise. There would be a dominant culture of evaluative thinking, using evidence formatively to inform design strategies. Information systems would be highly developed.

Prominent partnerships: Partners who previously might have been regarded as external will have become integral to learning systems, importantly including families, community bodies, enterprises, cultural institutions, universities, foundations and other learning environments. They would be active in shared learning leadership.

Flourishing assessment metrics and related accountability systems: A flourishing diversity of metrics will be in use to assess learning, reflecting the diverse aims of learning environments and wider systems to include mastery, understanding, the capacity to transfer knowledge, curiosity, creativity, teamwork and persistence. Quality assurance systems, including inspection, recognise successful learner engagement and the exercise of voice.

High levels of collaboration and networking: High levels of collaboration and engagement with partners, including other learning environments, will mean there will be flourishing, dense meso-level arrangements across districts, networks, chains and communities of practice. In a global world, it is common practice that such collaborative partnerships extend beyond national boundaries.

4.4 The future of the teaching profession

Scenarios are tools for helping to shape futures by stimulating reflection and action about the desirable and undesirable, the probable and the unlikely (OECD, 2006). They are not predictions and would never emerge in pure form. A recently-developed scenario set aims to stimulate reflection on the shape of future learning systems by asking who educators will be and where they will be located in, say, 2030 (Istance and Mackay, 2014). Will they be school-based or in many diverse educational locations for schooling? Will only teachers teach or will there be a high diversity of educators? Combining the extreme ends of these two dimensions gives the following four scenarios.

Scenario 1: *Teachers in educational monopolies*

Schools and teachers both dominate in this scenario. Teaching and learning are predominantly organised within places called schools, and though informal learning may take place at home or through media, there is very little non-formal organised teaching and learning. Certification and accreditation through education authorities are monopolistic, with rigorous control to ensure that no-one is establishing unauthorised educational programmes.

Scenario 2: *Specialist professionals as hubs in schools*

Schools also dominate in this scenario but this time with a wide range of adults and professionals engaged in teaching, such as volunteers, family members, community experts and specialists. Teachers, as those with specialist professional knowledge and certified status, are at the centre of the educational workforce and exercise strong professional leadership.

Scenario 3: **A system of licensed flexible expertise**

Instead of the "system" being defined in terms of institutions and places called schools, it is defined by who exercises responsibility for teaching. There is considerable flexibility and mobility in what teachers do and where they practice. This scenario implies significant investments in teacher preparation in continuing professional development and creating learning communities in an otherwise dispersed system, as schools are in the minority among educational destinations.

Scenario 4: In the open market

This is a de-schooling scenario in which those who teach are no longer required to possess formal teacher status. All kinds of other consultants and learning suppliers have come into the picture. There is a wide variety of learning locations of which only a minority are called "schools", including home schooling, tutoring, online programmes and community-based teaching and learning. It is a learning market, and it might be primarily about developing skills and capabilities demonstrable through a marketplace of different assessments.

TO FIND OUT MORE

Burns, T. and F. Köster (eds.) (2016), *Governing Education in a Complex World*, OECD Publishing, Paris, *http://dx.doi.org/10.1787/9789264255364-en*.

Istance. D. and A. Mackay (2014), *The Future of the Teaching Profession: A New Scenario Set*, Occasional Paper 138, Centre for Strategic Education, Melbourne.

OECD (2015a), "Growing and sustaining innovative learning environments", in *Education Policy Outlook 2015: Making Reforms Happen*, OECD Publishing, Paris, Chapter 8, *http://dx.doi.org/10.1787/9789264225442-12-en*.

OECD (2015b), *Schooling Redesigned: Towards Innovative Learning Systems*, OECD Publishing, Paris, *http://dx.doi.org/10.1787/9789264245914-en*.

OECD (2006), *Think Scenarios, Rethink Education*, OECD Publishing, Paris, *http://dx.doi.org/10.1787/9789264023642-en*.

Snyder, S. (2013), "The Simple, the Complicated, and the Complex: Educational Reform through the Lens of Complexity Theory", *OECD Education Working Papers*, No. 96, OECD Publishing, Paris, *http://dx.doi.org/10.1787/5k3txnpt1lnr-en*.

Zitter, I. and A. Hoeve (2012), "Hybrid learning environments: merging learning and work processes to facilitate knowledge integration and transitions", *OECD Education Working Papers*, No. 81, OECD Publishing, Paris, *http://dx.doi.org/10.1787/5k97785xwduf-en*.

TRANSFORMATION AND CHANGE IN LEARNING ECOSYSTEMS: THE TOOLS

Tool 4.1 *Explaining why our initiative will work.* This tool is designed for those who already have an innovation strategy or initiative in place. It gives a structure and terminology with which to interrogate the theory of action behind the strategy and how it is expected to lead to the desired innovation. It provides a way of communicating how the strategy works and of identifying improvements. This tool was developed through ILE work with a small set of systems dubbed "Laboratories of Learning Change".

Tool 4.2 *How advanced is our system towards the "7+3" framework?* This tool uses ILE indicators to interrogate how near or far your education system is from these signposts of innovation and change. It generates discussion about where priorities should lie in order to make most progress. It offers a way to take stock of the current situation prior to a more focused exercise of strategy design.

Tool 4.3 *How horizontally connected is our system?* This tool gives key stakeholders the means of mapping dynamic learning systems. It brings together the vertical levels and horizontal relationships. A main purpose of the tool is to raise awareness of the potential richness of connections and to acquire a more complete picture of existing learning providers and networks.

Tool 4.4 *Teachers in learning futures:* This tool invites users to think of future learning systems not only in terms of provision, programmes and technology, but of those who will be responsible for teaching and educating. It is a scenario tool for any group working towards big picture change in learning and education systems. It recognises that not all education for young people takes place in schools and not all those responsible as educators are formally-qualified teachers, and raises questions about where the ideal balances should be set.

Tool 4.1
Explaining why our initiative will work

This tool allows those working with a strategy to stand back to explain what it is aiming to do and how it works. It invites them to make explicit why the strategy is expected to make the hoped-for difference and will help expose whether the "theory of action" is under-developed or missing vital links. It will also help to sharpen the narrative behind the strategy.

Engage the key leaders of the strategy in this exercise. This works best when the team using the cards get feedback from others who are not directly involved in the strategy and who are therefore less likely to take design features or context for granted. This may be another team running a parallel strategy whose turn will come in the workshop to be interrogated; otherwise, use critical friends to help interrogate the diagram. The workshop can be significantly enhanced with good facilitation.

Constructing the flow diagram

The cards shown in Figure 4.3 are not meant to be exhaustive. We have included items from the ILE framework prominently among the cards. This is so that the strategy is explained in terms of learning change, leadership, pedagogy, educators, partnerships on the ground, networking and knowledge management and not only in such familiar programme terms as funding, duration, legislation, accountability requirements, etc. Please include whichever of these more conventional programme items you need.

Select those cards that are most relevant to your strategy – *you do not have to use all the cards*. Start with several of each one so that the same card may be used more than once. If a card is not relevant or only marginal, exclude it. You will also need markers and additional blank cards in case a key feature of your strategy cannot easily be described using the cards in the diagram.

> *Arrange the cards, in an order and with connecting arrows etc., in a way that best shows how the strategy works. Use a large display that can attach to a wall. Write briefly on each card how the heading on the card (e.g. "educator profiles" or "pedagogy") is being understood in the strategy (i.e. the content of the different components). You may add stickers to the arrows to explain the nature of the relationships the arrows signify.*

We expect this exercise to take time and not all will agree. *Its success relies upon careful preparation in advance* of the workshop to discuss the visual. The first completed diagram should be treated as a "draft" so be ready to return to work on it further before it is finalised.

Tool 4.1 Explaining why our initiative will work *(continued)*

Figure 4.3. Cards for building the diagram of a strategy's "theory of action"

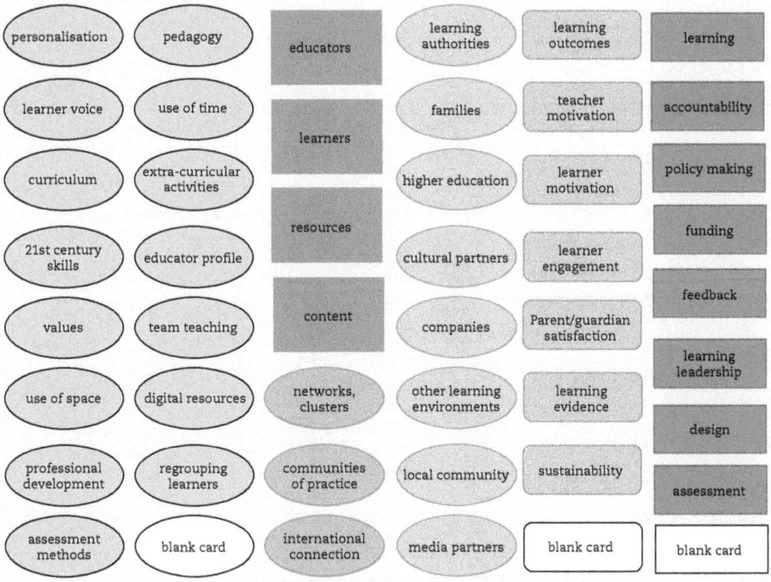

personalisation	pedagogy	educators	learning authorities	learning outcomes	learning
learner voice	use of time	learners	families	teacher motivation	accountability
curriculum	extra-curricular activities		higher education	learner motivation	policy making
21st century skills	educator profile	resources	cultural partners	learner engagement	funding
values	team teaching	content	companies	Parent/guardian satisfaction	feedback
use of space	digital resources	networks, clusters	other learning environments	learning evidence	learning leadership
professional development	regrouping learners	communities of practice	local community	sustainability	design
assessment methods	blank card	international connection	media partners	blank card	assessment
					blank card

Using the visual

Be ready to explain in a workshop:

- What is the focus of the strategy, how it works, and the main relationships and mechanisms involved?

- What is the "theory of action" underpinning the strategy? i.e. how the strategy is expected to reach its goals and how its impact will be sustained.

- The other participants should ask for clarifications and then discuss their impressions of how likely the strategy will work in the light of the explanations given. During this feedback the presenters should only listen and not respond.

- If the other workshop participants have prepared a similar chart because they are also responsible for an initiative/strategy, it is the turn of the next one and the roles are reversed.

Tool 4.1 Explaining why our initiative will work **(continued)**

- The teams are given time to digest the feedback and they then come back together. Each team explains what they heard in the feedback and how this has caused them to revise their original diagram. Each team should also explain the action that they consider now to take in the light of the feedback.

Getting the most from the visual

The value of presenting a strategy visually, in a way so as to be understood by those unfamiliar with it, is:

- **In preparation:** Moving beyond written texts and showing multiple relationships help to make assumptions explicit. It is also a means of seeing how far those working in a particular strategy share the same understanding about how it works.

- **In communication:** A wall chart with cards and arrows as a visual representation of a strategy significantly enhances the power of communication with others. The wall chart can be transferred into slideshow format.

- **As a record:** This form of presentation offers a means of recording perceptions of a strategy. Visuals may usefully capture the way that perceptions evolve (using, for instance, handheld devices).

The visual may simply be taken as a device to aid workshop discussion. Beyond this, the graphical representation may be further elaborated by drawing on the feedback received. Such post-workshop elaboration can be communicated to the wider community of practice and help to strengthen the strategy's narrative.

Tool 4.2
How advanced is our system towards the "7+3" framework?

The *Schooling Redesigned* report has proposed indicator areas that would show, assuming appropriate data existed, whether movement was taking place in systems of schooling in the directions identified by the ILE study.

The purpose of this tool is to use these indicator areas to interrogate how near or far your education system has moved in these directions. It is to generate discussion by influential stakeholders about where the strategic prioritising should occur in order to make most progress, or to help lay the ground for such design work.

Figure 4.4. Broad indicators for charting progress towards the ILE framework

Learning activity and motivation

Learners show high levels of engagement and persistence.

Schools and classrooms are characterised by the "buzz" of collegial activity and learning. A variety of sites for learning will be commonplace beyond conventional classrooms, including different forms of community learning.

Learner agency and voice

With more personalised learning, the learners become more powerful. They are clearly represented in learning leadership teams. They have agency and not only a formal voice.

Educator knowledge

Educators are familiar with the ILE Learning Principles. They understand the nature of learning and use diverse teaching strategies related to them. Professional knowledge is informed by research.

Educator views and practice

Teachers and other educators engage in professional discussion about learning strategies, within the organisation and in relation to individual learners. They also actively engage with learning leadership, innovation and there is widespread professional collaboration, including team teaching.

Inter-disciplinarity, curriculum development and new learning materials

Extensive work is taken to integrate inter-disciplinary knowledge around key concepts and to develop corresponding learning materials and pedagogies. There is flourishing research and development around pedagogical expertise and integrated content knowledge, and this is not monopolised by universities.

Mixed, personalised pedagogical practices

System-wide there is a rich mix and diversity of active pedagogical practices, including whole-class, small group and individual study. There is direct, virtual and blended learning, school- and community-based. Personalised approaches and formative assessment are highly visible.

Tool 4.2 How advanced is our system towards the "7+3" framework? *(continued)*

Digital resources, social media and innovative ICT use

Learners engage in research and intense exchanges around learning projects through social media and ICT.

Educators will connect with each other, with learners, and with other partners and networks. Teaching, learning and pedagogy will often be tech-rich.

Learning evidence and evaluation

Evaluative thinking and the use of evaluative evidence formatively to inform design strategies are common practice. Self-review and associated collaboration and reflection are visible forms of professional practice.

Diverse evaluation and assessment metrics

Diverse assessment metrics are developed and in widespread use. These reflect the aims of learning environments and include mastery, understanding, capacity to transfer knowledge, curiosity, creativity, teamwork and persistence. Assessment extends outside conventional school settings.

Quality assurance systems recognise successful learner engagement and the exercise of voice.

Sophisticated information systems and individual portfolios

The detailed profile and learning history of each learner will be readily accessible for all engaged in designing the teaching, strategy and the learning environment.

Leadership profiles

System-wide, there is a strong focus on learning and design. Decision-making will typically be shared among the professional community, learners, and other stakeholders, including foundations.

Diverse partners, highly visible

Partners become integral to pedagogical cores and formative learning leadership. Partners importantly include parents and other family members, but also community bodies, enterprises, cultural institutions, universities, and other learning environments.

Density of meso level activity

High levels of collaboration and engagement with partners, including other learning environments, mean a dense, visible meso level covering districts, networks, chains, and communities of practice.

Global connection

In a global world, it is common practice that partnership contacts, with other learning environments and different stakeholders, extend beyond national boundaries.

Tool 4.2 How advanced is our system towards the "7+3" framework? *(continued)*

- Discuss all the indicators with the whole group, and whether your current system seems near or far away from them taken as whole.

- Be more specific about each indicator area and why the participants believe that these are better or less well developed in the system. Divide them into those indicators which are already starting to describe your system and others that remain far from realised.

- Identify those lead indicators that, if in place, would suggest significantly desirable change in the system. Take time to discuss the reasons why these would be pivotal to change.

- Take between 1-3 of those indicators, and split into groups. Suggested foci for group discussion are:

  – What would be needed to make that change happen?

  – What would be needed to provide valid measures of these as indicators?

  – How movement towards this indicator would impact on your own school, network or community?

- Come back into the full group to consider how the whole-group and individual-group discussions should inform strategising in your system.

A possible follow-up exercise would take a similar number of the indicator areas that are furthest from being realised. In this case, the discussion can focus on the following topics:

- How important is it to move in this direction?

- Why is change so difficult?

- What might be done to unblock change?

Tool 4.3
How horizontally connected is our system?

This tool offers a way of describing learning arrangements beyond the conventional hierarchical characterisation of a school system and by recognising the importance of networks and clusters. It gives system designers a way of seeing how to develop the horizontal and networked aspect of the system; it gives networks, schools and other providers a way to locate themselves in a networked ecosystem.

This is suitable for workshop activity or for longer-term mapping. Use a grid as in Figure 4.5 and fill in the numbers of schools and districts with chosen symbols in the right-hand column, and devise a way to represent classes without flooding the diagram. Then begin to fill in the rest of the grid. This may be done using knowledge available around the workshop table or it may require more extensive research. Pay particular attention to:

- formal networks organised by the school system
- voluntary networks and communities of practice involving particular teachers or groups but not whole schools
- voluntary school networks
- networks and partnerships that involve non-formal partners
- non-formal providers
- official and voluntary networks of districts
- alliances and networks of the whole system within a country or internationally.

It will be impossible to do this comprehensively, but engaging in the exercise will meet a main purpose of the tool which is to raise awareness and acquire a much more complete picture of learning providers and networks. This by itself is important.

You may wish to work further with this grid in order to inform overall strategy and system policy. One way might be to add information about particular priority learning areas (e.g. STEM or leadership learning or social and emotional skills) in how they are covered by the different providers and networks. Another way would be to identify key gaps, differences, lack of connection, etc.

The policy question to be posed once the grid has been completed is:

- *What might we do to foster more effective connection and to grow the meso level?*

Tool 4.3 How horizontally connected is our system? *(continued)*

Figure 4.5. Weakly- and strongly-networked learning systems

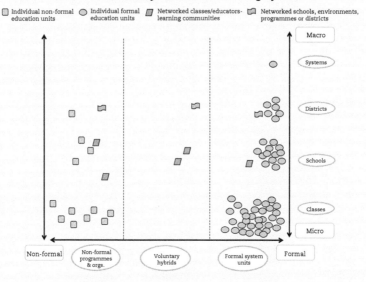

A vertical, weakly-connected learning system

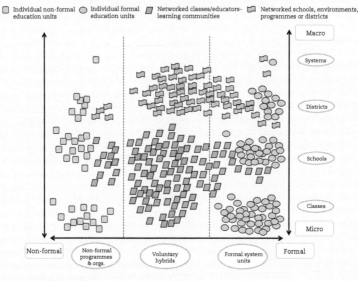

Strongly-networked learning system

Tool 4.4
Teachers in learning futures

Scenarios can be powerful tools in the armoury of those in decision-making and leadership positions in education. They can sharpen up viewpoints about possible, probable and desirable futures and help to set long-term direction. Scenarios are not predictions and none in their pure form would actually happen.

The purpose of this tool is to think of future learning systems not only in terms of provision, programmes and technology, but of those who will be responsible for teaching.

The tool assumes a workshop format. The workshop can begin with each participant reading the final section of the introductory overview to this chapter. Each participant then individually should:

a) choose their least and most preferred scenario (among *Teachers in Educational Monopolies*; *Specialist Professionals as Hubs*; *Licensed Flexible Expertise*; and *In the Open Market*) and in whole-group discussion say why

b) put a sticker somewhere on the 16-square grid (Figure 4.6 in large format) where each thinks the best scenario for 2030 should be located.

Break into four groups, one on each scenario. No-one should be allotted to their chosen favourite. Each group should identify three reasons why their allotted scenario might be a positive future (even though no-one started out enthusiastic about it).

Come back together, and each group should outline why the scenario they discussed has positive aspects. This should be followed by general discussion of the different scenarios and the reasons identified.

The participants should now revisit the original locations of their stickers and say whether they would leave it unchanged or move it and why.

The whole group can then discuss the ideal location for the future teacher profession anywhere on the grid on these two dimensions. That discussion might focus especially on:

• How near that is to the existing situation in your system.

• What other features of the teaching force not captured by these two dimensions should be elaborated in this ideal scenario.

• The changes that will be needed to make this ideal location come about.

Tool 4.4 Teachers in learning futures **(continued)**

Figure 4.6. **The future teacher scenario set**

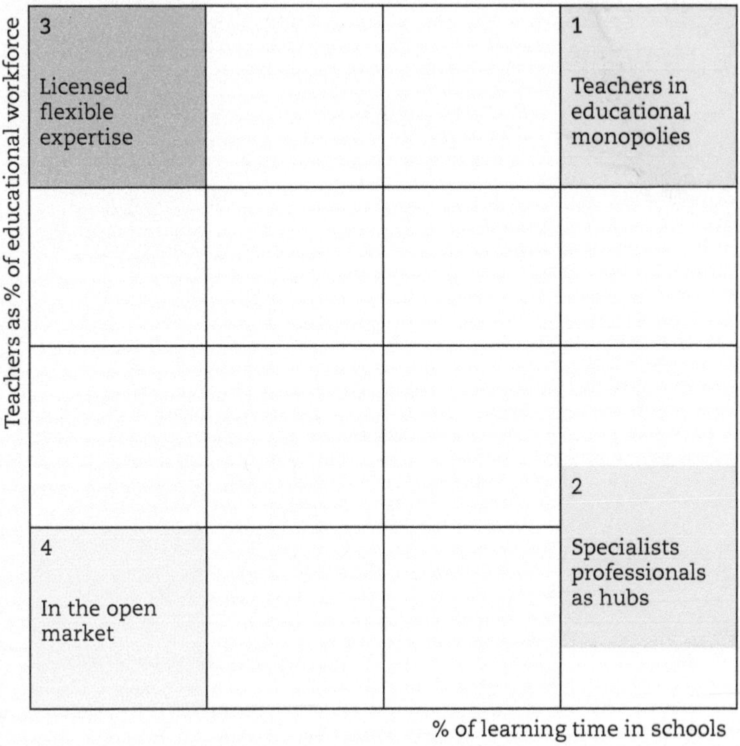

Source: Istance, D. and A. Mackay (2014), The Future of the Teaching Profession: A New Scenario Set, Occasional Paper 138, Centre for Strategic Education, Melbourne.

ORGANISATION FOR ECONOMIC CO-OPERATION AND DEVELOPMENT

The OECD is a unique forum where governments work together to address the economic, social and environmental challenges of globalisation. The OECD is also at the forefront of efforts to understand and to help governments respond to new developments and concerns, such as corporate governance, the information economy and the challenges of an ageing population. The Organisation provides a setting where governments can compare policy experiences, seek answers to common problems, identify good practice and work to co-ordinate domestic and international policies.

The OECD member countries are: Australia, Austria, Belgium, Canada, Chile, the Czech Republic, Denmark, Estonia, Finland, France, Germany, Greece, Hungary, Iceland, Ireland, Israel, Italy, Japan, Korea, Latvia, Luxembourg, Mexico, the Netherlands, New Zealand, Norway, Poland, Portugal, the Slovak Republic, Slovenia, Spain, Sweden, Switzerland, Turkey, the United Kingdom and the United States. The European Union takes part in the work of the OECD.

OECD Publishing disseminates widely the results of the Organisation's statistics gathering and research on economic, social and environmental issues, as well as the conventions, guidelines and standards agreed by its members.

OECD PUBLISHING, 2, rue André-Pascal, 75775 PARIS CEDEX 16
(96 2017 03 1 P) ISBN 978-92-64-27723-6 – 2017

Lightning Source UK Ltd.
Milton Keynes UK
UKHW020726280821
389620UK00002B/5

9 789264 277236